Blessings !
Cathy Catching

Guidebook
to
Angel Talk

Guidebook
to
Angel Talk

Learning to communicate with angels and other divine beings!

Cathy Catching

BALBOA.
PRESS

A DIVISION OF HAY HOUSE

Balboa Press books may be ordered through
booksellers or by contacting:

Balboa Press
A Division of Hay House
1663 Liberty Drive
Bloomington, IN 47403
www.balboapress.com
1 (877) 407-4847

Because of the dynamic nature of the Internet, any web
addresses or links contained in this book may have changed
since publication and may no longer be valid. The views
expressed in this work are solely those of the author and do
not necessarily reflect the views of the publisher, and the
publisher hereby disclaims any responsibility for them.

The author of this book does not dispense medical advice or prescribe
the use of any technique as a form of treatment for physical, emotional,
or medical problems without the advice of a physician, either directly
or indirectly. The intent of the author is only to offer information
of a general nature to help you in your quest for emotional and
spiritual well-being. In the event you use any of the information in
this book for yourself, which is your constitutional right, the author
and the publisher assume no responsibility for your actions.

Any people depicted in stock imagery provided by Thinkstock are
models, and such images are being used for illustrative purposes only.
Certain stock imagery © Thinkstock.

Print information available on the last page.

ISBN: 978-1-5043-6482-9 (sc)
ISBN: 978-1-5043-6483-6 (hc)
ISBN: 978-1-5043-6507-9 (e)

Library of Congress Control Number: 2016913809

Balboa Press rev. date: 09/02/2016

I would like to dedicate this book to the Supreme Being that I know as God. Although many call you by different names, I know that it makes no difference to You as the name is just a formality.

Thank you for sending in your amazing heavenly messengers that I know as angels to assist me in making this world a better place!

Table of Contents

Preface

Hi! My name is Cathy Catching and I am an angel intuitive with clairaudience as my strongest skill set. How I became a clairaudient intuitive is quite interesting and that story is included in my first book, *Angel Talk*. For those of you who have not read it, I will give you a brief synopsis. In October, 2011, I began hearing God's heavenly messengers in audible voices, inside and outside my head (I'll explain more about how this works a little later). Although I was a little startled in the beginning, I quickly realized that this was an amazing blessing and I let go of all my fears. A short time later, these remarkable voices provided the comfort and guidance that I needed when I experienced an absolutely extraordinary healing from an incurable muscle disorder!

After my healing, I realized the importance of divine communication and how it can help anyone navigate their way through life. This extraordinary information is available for everyone on how to experience happiness and good health; achieve prosperity; and how to live in peace and harmony with each other. I realized that the key to all of this lies within each and every one of us.

It is our choice (free will) as to whether we want to unlock what is available to us. How do we do this? The first step is to simply ask for help from a divine being of our choice. The second step is to make the necessary changes that we are guided to make. The final step is to have the faith that the divine world will deliver exactly what we need in perfect timing!

Although there are many books and articles available regarding divine communication, my angels urged me to teach others the methods that they taught me. It is always good to have as much information available and let the student decide which method works best for them.

Thus, *Guidebook to Angel Talk* was born!

To my angels:

Thank you for your love and support as I walk
this incredible journey with you.

I would also like to thank my friends and supporters
who have encouraged me to write this book.

Introduction

Although many of you will want to jump right into the meditation part of this book, hoping to immediately connect, try not to skip the first few chapters. This preparation work is really quite necessary to fully understand the messages that will be coming in. Plus, this information will help you in your day to day appreciation of all things around you!

This is a learning experience and there are steps that need to be taken and lessons to be learned. It is similar to taking a course at school. You will not know everything the first day nor would you be expected to. And like many courses, you can work at your own pace. Some will learn quickly and others will take awhile. Just trust that if the pace needs to be faster, your angels will make sure that it happens.

It is also important to understand that divine communication should be practiced daily to reap the greatest benefits. Just like physical exercise, "more effort equals greater reward". With this being said, though, my angels are telling me that some of you will be "kick-started" and may progress very rapidly!

Although intuition (pipeline to the divine world) is a natural gift that each of us has, complete understanding of how it works is not. Try not to be frustrated. Angels always know what is in our best interest and will guide us accordingly. We may not understand their methods, but it's important to trust them; stay positive; and be patient.

I fully believe that many of you are part of the "spiritual awakening" that began in the last few years. Some feared this was the end of the world and others believed it to be a year that marked a positive shift in consciousness. It's important to remember that it's really all about perspective. Keeping a positive outlook is a whole lot healthier than keeping a negative one.

For those that are interested, my first book, *Angel Talk*, recounts my own personal awakening (and physical healing) in great detail. My clairaudient gift began in October, 2011 and subsequent physical healing happened in November, 2011. For those of you interested in numbers and their significance, my healing encompassed the date 11-11-11. Yes, I thought it was really cool, too, and that is just one interesting little timing event that I covered in that book.

Anyway, I have also met other folks who recently experienced a major spiritual, emotional or physical change within their own lives and I find this very exciting for the future! I am being told that many people are being awakened so that they can do some incredibly phenomenal healing work on our planet. I am extraordinarily happy to be a part of this and want to teach as many people as possible what I have learned from my angels.

Heal thyself, then heal the world!

Chapter One

Angels 101

The word "angel" is derived from the Greek word "angelos" which means messenger. These beings have been described in almost every known culture since the beginning of recorded human history. Some of these celestial beings have been clearly described with wings and others with simply an ethereal glow about them. They are known as "God's messengers" and act as benevolent intermediaries between heaven and earth.

Although most people in today's world would describe an angel as appearing in human form with wings, this description is mainly so that we can identify them based on our own personal training. It is also for our benefit in that it is easier to identify with a being that looks like us. We are more amenable to them helping us and this image is an easy visual concept for us.

The appearance of wings also serves a purpose in that we naturally associate them with a physically higher level than us. Wings would allow them to fly over us and cross into what we perceive as heaven above us; thus lending credibility of their divineness.

Angels are actually beautiful and indescribable white light beings whose energy is unlimited. They have powers that are simply beyond our comprehension. These astonishing ethereal beings are with each of us all the time to guide us in our spiritual progression.

Let me explain. I believe that our soul is eternal and reincarnates into human form as many times as necessary until that soul reaches a perfect enlightenment. After that, the soul may continue to reincarnate to teach others their path to enlightenment or may work from the other side in various projects.

It is worth mentioning here that enlightenment and attaining a higher level of consciousness have various definitions and meanings. For the sake of this book, I will refer to this as "having gained advanced spiritual knowledge that allows one to be free from fear and realize that limitations are only within the mind."

Enlightened beings live their lives in a blessed state and are optimistic and full of positivity; live without fear and worry; and trust in a Universal Energy Source to take care of their earthly needs. Once they become enlightened, they understand the need to help others attain the same level of peace and happiness. By doing this, they are assisting mankind towards achieving complete peace and harmony.

Angelic guidance is always available but normally we have to request their help. There are times when they will communicate and intercede without the request but I have not been given details on when and why this happens. For the most part, people need to reach out and have the desire to grow spiritually before they can become really involved.

I think it is important to note here that another reason for them to want us to ask for their help is that it spurs us to look and listen for a response. If you are having a conversation with someone, you may not hear what they are entirely saying unless you are asking a question. It is your desire at that point to obtain a response and you normally pay more attention.

I believe that angels are here to help us with our divine encounters in a personal manner. They can present as male or female; and also with various personalities to assist us in what we need at the time. Many of you will understand this as you get to know your angels and will consider them to be your best of friends!

Each of us has a minimum of two assigned angels, although many people have more than that. One angel is what we consider our "guardian angel" and stays with us for our lifetime while on earth. I believe that this angel can change during our lifetime if circumstances warrant it.

One such circumstance is when a person's spiritual level rises and they become enlightened or "awakened to their divine gifts". I then believe that it is possible that a higher ranking angel steps in to become their guardian. Some enlightened ones are also considered lightworkers who have progressed to a higher level of spirituality.

It is their job to teach and perform healing work during their lifetime on earth. The healing work is done to help others to advance to a higher level of consciousness. In order to carry out these duties, these lightworkers need the assistance of these higher ranking angels. Many of them (if not all) have what we know as archangels as their guardian angels.

I might add that lightworkers are all healers, but not all healers are considered lightworkers. Some that are doing healing work still retain negativity within their lives and have a degree of egocentricity that impedes their progress. These folks have desire to help others but have a few issues to work out for themselves.

I have personally run into a few of these people myself. I recently met a lady that ran a healing shop that included holistic medicinal treatments. She was very pushy in her attempt to have me sample one of her recipes and became downright rude after I declined it. Although she would consider herself a healer, she was too caught up in her own ego to be considered a lightworker.

I am elaborating on this so that you will know that there are various degrees of healers out there. Please remember that in this respect, don't allow one bad apple to spoil the entire bunch. Many healers operate fully within love and light. They are full of loving messages without criticism or condemnation.

As I mentioned before, our guardian angel stays with us during our lifetime on earth. They are typically viewed as those angels that provide protection and comfort and may present as a "grandmotherly-type" presence. Many don't call upon them unless they are in an emotional or physical crisis, although they are here for all of our other needs as well. It is not necessary to request help from a particular angel although many people like this concept.

Most folks also want to know more about their guardian angel, including their name. If this appeals to you, just simply ask her or him to reveal what they would like for you to call them. Then, simply pay attention over the next few days and notice if a name keeps reappearing.

You may read the name somewhere or you may hear it repeatedly in person or over the radio or television. Pay attention to derivatives of the name as well. For example, if you hear the name "Isadora" one day and hear "Dora", "Dory", or "Izzy" a few more times over the next few days, you can be sure that you have the right name!

If it's important enough and the name is uncommon, someone could even say a word that rhymes with the name that they are trying to communicate to you. For example, the angels are trying to convey the name "Isadora" to you and you are at the grocery store. You hear the word "dizzy" yet you thought they said "Izzy" or someone mentions the word "door" yet you thought they said "Dora". This would be another way of clarification on what your angel would like you to call them.

The second assigned angel that each of us has is what I have been told is our "soul angel". This angel remains with our soul for all of eternity. I am speculating here, but feel that the reasoning behind having two angels is mainly for our emotional benefit. One angel is very capable of taking care of all our needs but I believe that most of us like the idea of having an angel on each side of us.

I also believe that the connection with a soul angel is also to introduce us to a different type of angel that is available to meet our daily needs. Our soul angel is there to provide daily advice and guidance that can greatly enhance our quality of life. With that being said, there are also archangels available to us for similar purposes and we can connect with them as well.

I believe that soul angels typically present with a more lighthearted personality than our guardian angels. I know that my own soul angel, Isabella, presents as a cheerful, loving female angel. She can help lift my mood with a few corny jokes as well as help me stay focused and motivated. Having a connection with your soul angel is like having a personal coach available to you at all times!

You can also request your soul angel to reveal his or her name by going through the same process as above. Just ask for them to reveal what they would like you to know them by and wait for a name to be revealed!

Guardian angels as well as soul angels can also be assisted by deceased loved ones or other deceased spirits that we may or may not have known. These spirits may have been assigned for this particular duty or they may have petitioned for the assignment.

I have been told that there is not a limit on how many deceased spirits can help us at any given time. These spirits are also allowed to help several people simultaneously. This lends credibility to how a deceased grandmother can be there for all of her children and grandchildren at the same time.

Other spirits that are allowed to assist us are known as "spirit guides" and "ascended masters". They are normally believed to have walked on earth in human form. Spirit guides were typically associated to be those spirits that assisted psychics with their work although this concept is changing. They can help all types of healers, including angel intuitives, energy healers, psychics, etc. They usually are described as being some sort of elder within their community with an important or noteworthy position.

They usually "present" themselves in full regalia that is typical of their culture. An example would be an Indian chief wearing a full ceremonial outfit including a headdress and other noticeable accessories. The adornment is what catches the attention of a psychic/intuitive/reader so that they are easily recognized.

Spirit guides can also present with some unusual physical characteristic that is unique. An example of this type of spirit guide would be the presentation of a hunched back person walking with the assistance of a tall stick or cane. Although he has minimal accessories, his unusual body shape and mannerisms (hobbling, etc.) will catch your attention.

Ascended masters are also allowed to help us here on earth. These spirit guides were also once human and were considered great healers, prophets or teachers of spiritual enlightenment while living. It is believed that they completed their Divine Plan here on earth and continue to do healing work from the realms of the spirit world.

Ascended masters include Jesus, the Virgin Mary (or Mother Mary), Buddha, as well as many other important spiritual beings. They come from many different cultures and can be from ancient or more modern times. In the beginning, you will probably make a connection with the ascended master that you would be most familiar with. As you progress, the divine world may introduce you to other beings that can help you in your journey.

Getting to know your guardian and/or soul angel (as well as any of the spirit guides) is important in that it gives you the comfort of knowing that you are never alone and establishes a very personal connection. It is very likely that you will also communicate with other types of angels, including the archangels.

There are many reference sources available about the archangels and the information is not all consistent. Don't be too concerned about how many there are or how to spell their names as this is not that important. You will be guided into a few sources of information at some point and just do your best to study what is available.

As they work with you, they will reveal who they are and what they want to teach you. I have included a chapter towards the end of this book on the archangels that I have studied and what I learned about them. Keep in mind that their connection and manner of presentation to you may be a little different than mine. They will build a personal connection with you in a way that you will understand.

There are many other types of angels with various duties but it can get quite complicated to go into them here. Some of you may advance into learning about these beings as well. For now, I recommend just asking to communicate in general and waiting to see who answers. The angels and/or other divine beings that you need the most will always be the ones that respond!

Chapter Two

Why Communicate?

Angels are here to assist us in living a life that is rewarding and full of love. They can also assist us in our daily lives with guidance and inspiration so that our life is happier. In doing this, they teach us how to heal our mind, body and soul by releasing all negativity and believing that all things are possible.

For some of you, they will even show you how you can make a positive difference in the world around you. Don't ever discount the power of your influence when your intention is based on love and healing!

Although the rest of this chapter gives an overview of the benefits of angelic communication, the healing aspect is quite complex. I will be elaborating on how the angels can help us heal in my next book, tentatively titled *"Healing with Angel Talk – How communication with angels can heal your mind, body and soul!"* I'm super excited about this one! I have been given great detail on how to teach others to heal from a variety of issues, including common ones such as muscle tension and headaches as well as complex issues surrounding post traumatic stress disorder (PTSD).

Many people on our planet have experienced emotional pain in some form or fashion. Angels are here to help us deal with this pain. Veterans, abuse victims and those who have suffered from any other kind of trauma can benefit from angelic communication. "We can help you overcome traumatic issues, no matter what the source!"

Generally, we tend to hold on to that pain and it creates problems for us (including health issues) during our life. Our angels can help us understand the circumstances on why that pain was experienced (if this is important) and what lessons were learned as a result. Many times, that pain becomes self-inflicted as we continue to dwell on it.

The angels have taught me that it is not in our best interest to focus on the negativity of an event or situation as then we can't move past it. Letting go of it is of utmost importance in our healing. Often times, the letting go or releasing of the pain is complicated because of emotions that are involved. Guilt, anger and resentment (grudges) are a few of the biggest culprits that hold us back from our emotional healing.

I wasn't going to go into detail about this but I am being guided to briefly discuss grudges. Holding a grudge against someone is never in our best interest. Our angels encourage us to offer forgiveness to all that have offended us, no matter how big the offense. Forgiveness is not about condoning or excusing the offense, but simply letting it go. By offering this forgiveness, we free ourselves of the cumbersome burden of a grudge and allow our hearts to be filled with love.

Negative thinking in general is also not good for us and our angels want us to change it. The negative thought process creates frustration and adds to our disappointment. Frustration can turn into anger and disappointment can develop into depression. Our entire outlook can go sour and we may feel that life has no meaning and no purpose. This is absolutely not true as we all have a purpose when we enter this earth.

Negative thinking also contributes to poor health by creating negative chemicals for our body and impairing the good ones that are trying to keep us healthy. Our angels are here to help us develop a positive outlook so that we are physically healthier. Just remember that the mind and body are closely connected!

They also would like us to take good care of our bodies and can guide us into what we need. Many have difficulties with poor eating habits. The angels can assist us by guiding us into good foods and away from harmful ones. Cravings for medicinal foods can spontaneously occur and unhealthy foods can suddenly become less palatable.

Exercise is always encouraged by the angelic realm as this is in everyone's best interest. They have the utmost compassion for us and understand that this can be difficult to achieve with a busy schedule. They assist us with this by helping us "stumble" into a class that we would enjoy or gently remind us to take the stairs when possible. Many times they will help us get additional exercise without our even being aware of it!

Angels also want us to communicate with them so that we can heal our soul. They are trying to teach us about them and their role in our lives. They want us to learn about their unconditional love and how to improve our spiritual connection.

Many have encountered some form of religious indoctrination that they felt was too conditional or hypocritical so they turned away. Angels are here to help us heal this disconnect into a more rewarding relationship with the spirit world.

They also want us to have faith in them and the loving Universal Energy Source that created them. He has been known by a multitude of names; depending on location, language and time period; and is not picky about how you refer to Him. Throughout my writings, though, I also refer to this supernatural being as God, The Maker and Supreme Being as these are the names that I have learned.

Angels are also trying their best to teach us to "think outside the box" and to not limit ourselves. I believe that our only limitation is the ego part of our mind. This is the part of the mind that is based on logic and reasoning and is developed through our learned experiences and training on earth.

They don't want us to discount this information, but incorporate it into our spiritual mind. While learning to meditate, though, it is important to turn the ego off so that the angels can deliver their messages. I have coined the term "egobegone" (ego-be-gone) which can be said several times before a meditation session to help one in their communication.

Saying this repeatedly distracts the conscious mind (the one that may be thinking about the grocery list) and helps the brain waves shift into a meditative state. It serves a similar purpose as meditative chants and songs or repetitive prayers.

Angels can also help us heal by teaching us how to connect with our departed loved ones. They can assist us in finding closure with them by allowing us to "see" or "feel" where they are and what they are doing. They can also facilitate communication with them so that we can continue a relationship if so desired and if it is in our best interest to do so.

In addition to healing our mind, body and soul, angels are available for daily guidance and inspiration. It is this daily guidance that can steer us into the best parking place (if our exercise requirements have been met); remind us of things that we have forgotten; help us with our parenting skills or anything else you can imagine! They can inspire us to clear out clutter within our home and show us how to do so without becoming overwhelmed. They can also ignite our creative side which can be very rewarding and prosperous!

And, if all of that isn't enough, communicating with these wonderful beings can help us become healers, whether in traditional or non-traditional lines of work. I believe that every so often, people are "awakened" to help heal our planet. They begin to have an increase in psychic and other supernatural types of experiences, including premonitions.

I believe that these awakenings are cyclical and happen when mankind is ready for the next phase of spiritual progression. This "tuning up" of the world occurs after a certain number of individuals reach their personal level of attunement and become the lightworkers that I mentioned earlier.

These lightworkers then spread healing messages of love and peace throughout the world which is what the angels want. "Your world is in need of healers from all walks of life. Many are being awakened so that they can carry out divine work!"

Personally, I believe that many of you reading this book are being trained as we speak to become the lightworkers that our world needs!

Chapter Three

Methods of Communication

There are a number of ways that angels will communicate with us and I will address the ones that I know of in this chapter. Before we begin, though, it is important to understand the definitions of the "mind's eye" and "impression" so that you will know what I'm referring to a little later.

The "mind's eye" is a term associated with our brain's ability to visualize something. It is closely associated with our memory and imagination but can also be influenced by a supernatural source, such as your angels.

The "mind's eye" can "see" images with the eyes closed or open. These visual images can be in color or black and white; can be still as in photographs or in motion as in movies; and can be vague or very detailed. Some of you may discount the information being received as real and think it's just imaginary. This is a normal part of the learning process. In time, you will be able to discern the difference.

A quick practice of using the mind's eye would be to close your eyes and visualize what your front door looks like. Look at it closely and notice all of the details about it. Where is the door handle/knob located? What color is the door? Now, open the door and walk inside, paying attention to all the details that you can remember about the inside of your home.

If this exercise is difficult or the information is fuzzy, then it is possible that you are not paying close enough attention to the world around you. Many times people become so preoccupied that they are not paying attention to their surroundings. Have you ever exited the mall or a grocery store and couldn't remember where you parked? Well, I know that I have!

It is important to do your best to "live in the moment" and absorb as much detail about your surroundings as possible. This will help your mind's eye become very sharp. With practice (and skills learned in the next chapter), you will find that angelic information is easier to understand. At some point, you will not need to close your eyes to be able to "see" the information.

I might also add here that you might see yourself as an observer (outside observer) watching yourself open the door rather than being the participant who actually opens the door. You might even toggle back and forth. I frequently see myself in both positions.

It may be meaningful at some point as to whether you are the outside observer or the participant but don't worry about it if it happens. Many times the angels will help us in our healing by directing us to become the outside observer in a situation so the practice is useful.

Angels commonly send information through the "mind's eye" by triggering a memory of something that you have seen, learned or experienced. These memories can also be relevant to what is currently going on in your life and will be useful to you. I'll explain more about this a little later as it can get quite detailed.

They can also send images that we are not familiar with. If you receive images like this, just write them down and date it as they are probably prophetic. They can be in the form of pictures, dates, diagrams, drawings, etc. I sometimes "see" or dream of people's faces that I don't know and will subsequently meet them. The meeting is not always important, but is sometimes practice in sharpening my skills. I now tend to pay more attention to the details about people's faces.

The definition of impression for this book is "an overall perception in the mind of an experience; it can include visual images within the 'mind's eye,' thoughts, feelings, sounds, smells, and tastes." In other words, the impression can include information that is normally gathered by your five senses.

Angels don't usually deliver information to us that can be perceived by all of our senses at one time as it can be overwhelming. Your personal experiences will vary, but the most common type of communication is through our thoughts and feelings.

These impressions are categorized according to how we perceive them. You are probably somewhat familiar with the terms claircognizance, clairvoyance, clairsentience and clairaudience but I will explain them a bit more in detail. There are also other categories; clairalience and clairgustance; that are less commonly discussed. All of these are what is known as our metaphysical senses or can be lumped together under the term "sixth sense".

As you study these definitions, many of you will realize that you have already been in communication with the divine world at some level. You will most likely gravitate towards one specialty area of communication, but you can become quite proficient at all of them!

Claircognizance is the ability to receive divine information in the form of knowledge that has not been learned. It is also referred to as "clear knowing". An example would be to know someone's name without being told. One who receives information in this manner is known as a claircognizant.

Clairvoyance is the ability to receive divine information in the form of visual images that are perceived in the mind's eye. It is also referred to as "clear seeing". An example would be to "see" a piece of fruit in your mind's eye without it actually being present. One who receives information in this manner is known as a clairvoyant.

Clairsentience is the ability to receive divine information through a feeling or sensation without being subjected to a catalyst for the feeling. It is also referred to as "clear feeling". An example would be to experience an emotion that someone else is having without there being a cause for it. Another example would be to experience physical chills or goosebumps that are unrelated to temperature change. This is a common method for angels and deceased loved ones to communicate. One who receives information in this manner is known as a clairsentient or an empath.

Clairaudience is the ability to receive divine information in an auditory manner. It can be either within the head (similar to hearing your own thoughts) or outside the ear (as if someone is in the room with you). An example of this is hearing your name called when there is no one around or hearing music without a source for it. Anyone that receives information in this manner is known as a clairaudient.

Clairalience is a term that is not used very often but is experienced quite frequently. It is defined as "clear smelling" and involves the ability to experience smells without a physical substance present. It is quite common for people to report smelling cigarette or tobacco smoke, perfumes or flower scents without any of those things being present. The smells are frequently associated with departed loved ones. Anyone who has this experience is considered to be clairalient.

Clairgustance, another term that is not used often, is the ability to perceive tastes without placing anything in the mouth or on the tongue and is considered "clear tasting". It is an unusual ability that I believe is not very common. I have met many intuitives but only one person who had this gift. If memory serves me correct, he once tasted a candy decoration that usually goes on cakes and this triggered discussion about a birthday/celebration. He would be known as a clairgustant if this was his strongest gift or he could be said to have clairgustant experiences.

Angels also convey information to us in a variety of other ways which would fall under the category of signs. Some people believe that signs are just coincidences, but they are definitely not. These include, but are not limited to, numbers (particularly repetition or patterns); songs/music; billboards; feathers; coins; birds of all kinds; dragonflies and butterflies.

The angels help draw our attention to these signs so that we can receive the messages. Sometimes these messages are very general and are provided with reassurance of their presence whereas other times, the signs are very specific. The timing of these signs is usually significant as they appear when we most need comfort or a particular message.

One other way that angels will communicate with us is through our bodies. I know this will sound strange to some of you but they can assist us in our body movements. I have had this happen on a few different instances that I recognized and found it to be a phenomenal experience.

Now that you have a better understanding of how the divine world connects with us, we will begin our preparation work! Don't skip past the next chapter as it is very valuable!

Chapter Four

Preparation - Don't Skip This!

Before beginning your angelic communication, it is important to do a little preparation work. This work involves sharpening the five senses that we are most familiar with. By doing this, the information that is delivered through your "sixth sense" is much easier to receive. It is recommended that you practice these experiences with a variety of objects and sounds to gain a better overall understanding.

Seeing – look at an object that is colorful and full of texture. You can use pictures at some point, but looking at an object three dimensionally is recommended at first. Study the details and take a mental picture of it as if you will have to describe it later. You can also describe it to yourself while looking at it.

It is also useful to think about what else it looks like to you. What thought "pops" into your mind as you look at it? Many times, the angels will guide us to look at something that will trigger another thought.

25

As an example, I once studied a red hibiscus flower in my back yard. It was fully open and reddish-orange in color. Inside the flower were several stamens (I think that's what they are called) that were yellow in color and had some sort of appendages off of them that were fuzzy with pollen. At the very top of the stamen were unusual looking caps that were bright red.

As I looked at the inside of it, I thought about how each of those appendages looked like terminals at a space station or airport, just waiting for an insect to land. Studying the detail of this flower helped me to fully appreciate its beauty (which is relaxing) and I now have a vivid picture of it filed away in my brain.

I actually photographed this flower for a photography class assignment and called it the "B-Terminal". Yes, I do believe that was a bit of channeled angel humor!

Many times people look at something without really seeing it as they are too preoccupied. By completing this type of exercise, you are fully absorbing what you are looking at (living in the moment). Angels want us to appreciate the visual beauty around us (which relaxes us) and studying the detail can trigger all kinds of positive brain activity (sharpens the brain).

Also, when we look at objects with any kind of color, we are receiving a type of color therapy. The various colors can stimulate certain chemicals within the brain and create a variety of responses. Studies have been done on this modality of healing and can be quite interesting to read up on.

For example, the color blue is known to relax most people and is sometimes used in the waiting rooms of doctor's offices and hospitals. The color red is considered a stimulating color that can signal excitement or a form of danger. Red is commonly associated with fire trucks and stop signs, both of which signal us to pay immediate attention. It is also important to note that we are not only affected by the colors themselves, but our learned associations with them.

I am oversimplifying most of this as the study of colors and how they affect us is quite complex. Just keep in mind that they do affect our emotional and physical state. During your exercise, you might try looking at several different colored objects and determine how you feel as you look at them.

The last major benefit for studying the details of objects is simply for our enjoyment. Our angels want us to slow down and appreciate what is around us so that we can be happier. I am always being encouraged to go outside more and enjoy the beauty of the outdoors. It is a natural and relaxing atmosphere that provides us the perfect place to decompress!

Smelling – find something that has an aroma that you like and hold it under your nose. This can be a flower, a spice, a perfume or anything that is easy for you to get to. Inhale the aroma a few times and pay full attention to it. Think about how you would describe it. Is it a strong or light fragrance? Does it smell sweet or sour? Is it fruity, floral or woodsy?

While doing this exercise, also pay attention to the way you feel. Smells have a strong link to memory and can trigger emotions or physical responses associated with that memory. These emotions and physical responses can surprise us as they can be very strong. Our brain stores all kinds of information from our experiences.

For this exercise, I decided to smell fresh coffee as it is one of my favorite smells. Since I like the darker roasted variety, my coffee smelled bold and rich. I detected a slightly nutty fragrance but couldn't really discern the rest of the aroma.

The smell of coffee always creates a general sense of well-being for me. I quickly become relaxed, calm and reflective. For me, the smell triggers all kinds of pleasant memories, from childhood to adulthood. In addition to memory triggers, research has shown that the smell of coffee stimulates a part of the brain that increases our sense of pleasure.

Smelling coffee also stimulates the part of the brain that helps us wake up even without ingesting it! This is beneficial for those (like me) who cannot tolerate much caffeine.

While on this subject, my angels would like me to caution you that caffeine, as well as other natural stimulants, are included in many energy drinks and diet foods so please read the labels carefully. Among other things, these stimulants can act as diuretics and can increase blood pressure and heart rate. I would also like to add that some people are much more sensitive to the effects of these stimulants and should completely avoid them.

Ingesting too much of any of them can create medical problems that can be life threatening. Many of these substances are not regulated and are easily available to all ages. They can be purchased at the corner convenience store or at the grocery store without difficulty and where there is no adult supervision.

Until these drinks become regulated, please teach your children about the dangers of too much caffeine and to avoid all energy drinks. It is best to teach them natural ways to gain more energy such as exercising and movement in general. It is also important for them to know that a positive attitude and happy mood serve as great catalysts for physical energy, too!

Okay, now that the angel's public service announcement is done, I'll get back to topic!

Paying attention and understanding smells can be beneficial in a number of ways. It helps us be alert to danger or unhealthy substances, such as toxins in the air or rancid foods. Smells also enhance our mealtime pleasure as the sense of smell and taste are closely related. Smells are also used as a method of healing known as aromatherapy.

I won't go into too much detail here but aromatherapy is an important avenue of healing. There are many fragrances/aromas that cause the body to release chemicals that are considered medicinal. An example would be the inhalation of lavender. This smell stimulates the part of the brain associated with sedation so it is commonly used for anxiety or sleep issues.

If you are having trouble with your sense of smell, it could be due to external sources. Medications, cigarettes and other environmental pollutants are known to cause interference with the olfactory system. Try to avoid what you have control over and recognize that these substances are affecting an important part of your brain.

As you work with your angels, they will guide you in understanding the importance of smells and how they personally relate to you. My angels know how much I love the smell of coffee and have sent me that aroma on a few mornings when it was important for me to get up! They know that this will work for me every time!

Tasting - at your next meal, sample each dish individually. Pay close attention to the texture, temperature and flavor as you chew. Is it soft, hard, warm, creamy, crumbly, crispy, fluffy, doughy, sticky, fatty, greasy? Is it sweet, sour, cold, salty, bitter, mellow, spicy? These are just a few words to describe how foods taste so if other words "pop" into your mind, use your own descriptions.

My personal experience with this exercise is when I ate something that was very fatty. I immediately noticed that my tongue felt unusual and realized that the fat was coating it and disrupting the flavor of the food. I then realized that the fat coating my tongue would have to be "rubbed off" by other foods and wondered how it would be processed inside my body.

I realized that at my normal body temperature, certain fatty foods would not be processed and that it would take an elevation of body temperature (and other factors) to eliminate these unwanted fats. This is just one reason why exercise is so important.

Just imagine a clogged drain and what it takes to open it up. If enough fat and debris get into those pipes, a plumber may need to be called and it can be quite costly. As far as the body is concerned, most of us know that eating too many unhealthy fats causes a multitude of problems, including obesity, diabetes, hypertension and cardiovascular disease.

I also had a similar experience when I ate something very salty. It must have overwhelmed my taste buds as my tongue went slightly numb and I couldn't completely taste all of the other foods. This was nature's way of telling me that the food was not good for me.

Too much salt has many adverse health effects, including hypertension and cancers. Fast foods and preserved foods are heavily laden with salt and should be avoided. So are many prepackaged foods found in the interior of the grocery store. I recommend shopping the perimeter of the store where the fresh and frozen foods are located.

I have a good friend who was diagnosed with stomach cancer a few years back. He did not smoke or drink; exercised regularly; had a positive outlook on life; and was at an optimal weight. He ate what he thought were healthy choices but most of his meals came from restaurants and fast food establishments. I believe that it was these meals that created the cancer in his stomach, so please be cautious about your food choices.

While discussing salt, it is important to understand that our taste buds can become accustomed to it or actually desensitized by it. If we avoid extra salt, our taste buds will readjust and be able to send out the appropriate warning signals to the brain of an excess. This holds true for sugar as well.

There are other ways to enhance the flavor of our food so that we completely enjoy it. Try a variety of natural spices to replace the added salt. Interestingly enough, lemon and salt affect the tongue in similar manners even though they are sour and salty. They send signals to the brain which perceives the food as salty. So, next time you get ready to salt that dish, add lemon instead!

Getting in touch with your sense of taste can be very important during angelic communication. The angels can help guide us into healthy foods and away from unhealthy foods. They can also help us crave the foods that we need for our own personal medicinal benefit. As in the examples above, I was guided to be cautious about how much fat and salt I was consuming so I paid more attention to my diet.

Another important point to make here is that it is difficult to receive the message from our angels if we are eating our food too fast or talking too much during a meal. It is important to ingest our food slowly and completely chew it up to receive the best benefits from the food and any potential information from our angels.

Eating slowly also helps our brain "catch up" to the internal nerve signals that our stomach is communicating to it. Our feeling of fullness or satiety is determined by these nerve signals and eating too fast can cause us to overeat as the signal has not arrived at the brain yet. There are also certain foods that help keep us full longer. Paying attention to your angel guidance will lead you into these foods if you are having difficulty losing weight due to overeating.

Another benefit to fine-tuning our sense of taste is in developing the gift of clairgustance. I mentioned this briefly in the previous chapter and defined it as "clear tasting". I believe that we will see an increase in folks with this gift in the near future as a new wave of intuitives are being schooled in this.

Communication through the sense of taste can help us with our own dietary needs or in counseling others through personal sessions. A skilled clairgustant can "taste" what the other person is eating too much or too little of and can advise them accordingly.

This gift can also be useful when a deceased loved one is trying to connect. An intuitive may taste a dessert that had special meaning for the deceased person. This would be considered a direct connection, whereby the reader mentions the taste and the client knows who is coming through.

The taste could also be indirect as well. As I mentioned earlier, the taste of a dessert, such as cake, can trigger a discussion of a birthday. This may lead into dialogue about the loved one who would have recently celebrated a birthday or there was something significant about the date for them.

Touching – for this exercise, I recommend that you find an object that has texture to it and one that is soft and smooth. The sense of touch can be very powerful and the angels want us to get in touch with it (their words, not mineJ)

Pick up the textured item and focus your thoughts on how it feels in your hand. Pay attention to whether it has any sharp points or rounded edges. Is it jagged, bumpy, coarse, scaly? Does it feel scratchy, feathery, hairy, spongy, fuzzy?

Let your fingers study the detail of the object. This skill can be quite useful in everyday life. Sometimes our eyes miss the flaws or cracks that are present in items that our sense of touch will not. I use this sense quite often when inspecting items for resale.

Also, pay attention to how you feel as your hands study the object. Are you calm and relaxed or do you feel invigorated and stimulated?

Now, pick up the smooth object and study the details with your hands. Is it rigid or malleable? Soft or firm? Satiny or velvety?

Here again, pay close attention to how you feel as your hands study this object. Are you calm and relaxed or do you feel invigorated and stimulated?

Tactile stimulation can have various affects on us depending on what our skin is touching. There are other factors involved such as temperature of the item and how fast the movement is but I won't go over that here.

What is important to share in this book is how these two items affect us differently. Most of you will notice that the item with texture does not promote calmness. You may not recognize it as stimulating but that is exactly what it does.

This is an innate ability to help us in perceiving imminent danger. An example would be to notice that while touching an object with certain textures, our bodies tend to tense up. This is because objects with uneven texture send certain nerve signals to the brain that alert us to the possibility of an injury. We are then on high alert as sharp objects can penetrate our skin. It is a protective mechanism built into our amazing body!

The opposite effect occurs when we touch most soft and smooth objects. Nerve signals are sent to our brain and it perceives these objects to be safe and comforting. As a consequence, feelings of comfort and safety emerge and our body responds accordingly by relaxing. Temperature is also an important factor as we respond more favorably to warm smooth objects rather than cold smooth objects.

I found it interesting that when I looked up synonyms (same meaning) for the word smooth, I found words such as peaceful, fluid, gentle, quiet and serene. In contrast, the antonyms (opposite meaning) for the word smooth were agitated, excited, broken, turbulent and troubled.

With the understanding of how important our sense of touch is, we can actively use touch therapy as a way to alleviate tension and stress. The key is to find something that you like and focus on how it feels and your brain will provide your relaxation chemicals!

This is why many people carry small polished rocks with them as their "worry stones". As they rub the smooth stones, tiny nerve impulses make their way to the brain which sends out a chemical that is calming. Thus, they are helping to alleviate their worries by promoting calmness.

They are also burning off excess stress chemicals by the repetitive motion (a minor form of exercise). The only drawback is that the stone does not always stimulate the pleasure centers of the brain that much. Also, if one does not entirely release the worry, it can return.

Touching soft and smooth fabric does stimulate the pleasure center of the brain and is another way for us to promote relaxation. It is the method of touch therapy that I would recommend. Silk, satin and velvet-like fabrics are very pleasing to our tactile sense but there are others that work just as well. It's easy enough to find a decorative pillow that has just that right "feel" to it. If you ask your angels for help, you might even find one that matches your décor!

Understanding how our tactile sense affects us will be important when we move into the next chapter and learn how to meditate!

Hearing – find some instrumental music that is appealing to you. Begin this exercise by just listening to one song and enjoying the experience. Then listen to it again and focus a few moments on one instrument. Try to focus on that one instrument by itself and listen to the part it plays in the overall song. Repeat this process, listening to each instrument individually.

I practiced this particular technique when I first became clairaudient. I could hear several angels talking to me at the same time in different vocal ranges and various tempos. I focused on each voice individually and could determine what they were saying and how fast they were talking. I remember comparing their voices to the different instruments in a symphony.

With a little practice, I could actually discern five different voices communicating with me! I knew intuitively that there were many more, but my brain and expertise level could only hear the five.

To better hear the angels, I listened to a fan that was sitting beside my bed. It provided white noise which was beneficial in a couple of ways. The white noise created positive brain wave activity that led to relaxation. It also helped me to determine that I was actually hearing voices. White noise provided the same continuous sounds so I knew that anything outside that spectrum was external.

I am now aware that listening to white noise also helps condition the auditory nerve for clairaudience. The angels know that constant sounds can be overwhelming for the human brain to handle. Therefore, if it is in someone's best interest to become clairaudient, the angels will essentially train their brains to be receptive!

The best way to understand why our auditory nerve needs to be conditioned is by a simple analogy. If you were to step out of a sound proof room and go directly into a very loud concert, you would gauge the music to be very loud and it might cause you nervous or physical distress. If you walk down a hallway towards the concert and can hear it get louder incrementally, you would probably not perceive it to be as loud even if the decibel level is the same.

I believe that many have recently become clairaudient and many more will do so. Practicing the previously mentioned exercise will help those in achieving this wonderful gift! By the way, if you are experiencing any kind of tinnitus or ringing in the ears, you may just well be on your way to hearing your angels!

It is also important to not be afraid. If you are experiencing fear because of societal beliefs or any other reason, just say a prayer. You will get comfort either immediately through a feeling or will be guided into more information that will help you process what is going on.

Now, we'll get back to the original exercise of listening to music. Besides trying to determine the different instruments, pay attention to the overall beat. Describe how the music sounds to you. Is it slow, melancholy, spiritual, jazzy? Is it upbeat, rhythmic, light, uplifting?

Also, pay attention to how it makes you feel. Does it make you want to take a nap or get up and dance? Do you feel blue or happy as you listen?

What is important is to pay attention to how different types of music impact how we feel. Music has a powerful affect on us whether we believe it or not. With that knowledge, we can then decide what to expose ourselves to. If we know that a melancholy song contributes to feelings of sadness, then we should avoid listening to it.

We should also do our best to always supervise our children in what music they are listening to. Be aware that there is music out there that contributes to teenage unrest and can easily incite them. Although we cannot control what they do when we are not around, we can give them the education about music that they need. Just remember that knowledge is power and will enable them to make good decisions.

My angels would also like me to caution folks about what music they play when young children are around. You may not think that they are paying attention to it, but they are absorbing something from it. Just remember that their nervous system is still young. Over stimulation from music can create unrest in small children as well. I think that parents sometimes forget this while listening to music on the radio in their vehicles.

Lyrics, as well, play a role in how a song affects us. Pay close attention to various songs and listen to the lyrics. Sometimes they are hard to hear so I occasionally look them up online. There are a few songs that I love the music to but am not fond of the messages that are being delivered through the lyrics.

We should always focus on listening to music with positive lyrics as this helps us stay in a positive frame of mind. Remember that positive thinking creates positive brain chemicals that improve our mood and physical health! In contrast, listening to negative lyrics can bring our mood down by creating those negative brain chemicals.

Developing good listening skills to the sounds around us is an important part of our angelic communication. Even if you don't become fully clairaudient, you may sometimes hear a message that is woven into another sound. An example would be to hear a word or sentence while listening to music that is not a part of the song.

The angels will also help our ears to "perk up" when they want us to take notice. It's as if the sounds get louder or we suddenly take notice in them. Don't worry if you feel like you missed the message as they will always repeat it for you.

I know that this section is rather lengthy but my angels would like me to briefly cover sound therapy before closing. It is widely understood that sound therapy can soothe us and an example would be how lullabies help babies to sleep.

What is not commonly understood is how certain tones can affect us. I am not well versed on this matter but am researching it. What I do understand is that my angels "played" a certain tone for me when I was having difficulty falling asleep. I'm assuming that it created a change in my brain wave activity that helped me sleep.

I believe that tone therapy will be increasing in the future as another modality of healing. It is really not a new concept but just introduced from a different angle. Tibetan singing bowls (a type of standing bell) have been around a long time and have been used to create healing tones for meditation.

There is also indication that various tones can heal our physical bodies. I believe that this will also become a more prominent form of healing in the near future. Of course, this naturally leads me into wanting to discuss frequencies and vibration but I will have to save that for another book!

After practicing all of the exercises in this chapter, you will find that your regular senses have been greatly sharpened. Just remember that your brain is like a massive computer where everything that you have seen, smelled, touched, tasted or heard is stored. Your angels can help you retrieve any of these experiences, even if you think you have forgotten them.

Sharpening your senses not only helps in angelic communication, but will aid you in everyday matters. It will be easier to recall details of things that you have seen or experienced; will enhance your communication skills with other people; and increase your overall enjoyment of life.

Chapter Five

Learning to Meditate

Now that you have polished all of your senses, let's work on learning how to meditate. Meditation is not really difficult and is crucial in communicating with your angels as well as staying physically healthy. As a matter of fact, science is showing that people who meditate live longer!

Meditation involves a process of mentally disconnecting from the physical world and connecting with the divine realm. For clarity, meditation does not require one to be free of all thoughts as this is impossible to do.

There are many ways to meditate and it is always a good idea to find the method that works best for you. Ultimately, we want to achieve a state of bliss or euphoria where we feel the connection between us and that heavenly divine world! There are also various stages of meditation, depending on what your intention is. Light meditation is good and can be practiced in most any environment to simply relax; intermediate meditation is useful when we have a bit more time to focus; and deep meditation is useful when we want to completely disconnect from our present world.

For the most part, I believe that my meditations fall into the second group, although I have experienced other levels. Once you understand how to meditate, you will begin to experience different levels based on how much time you have and what your intention is. What is important is to not judge your capabilities and keep trying even if you feel that you are not getting your desired results. Some of this just takes practice.

On a side note, when you are in deep meditation, you may lose awareness of your surroundings. This can feel rather strange in the beginning as you may feel like you are actually somewhere else. This is considered an out-of-body experience.

You can also experience very vivid visual images in this state and they can be three dimensional. I experience this on occasion and it can be a little startling in the beginning. A three dimensional visual image means that you can perceive depth as well as height and width. If you have ever been to a 3-D movie, you will understand the difference. I have requested that my angels only send 3-D visual images when I am very still as I tend to experience motion sickness rather easily.

My favorite form of meditation is called "mindfulness meditation" and can be practiced even in a noisy environment. The goal of this meditation is to be fully in the present moment, whereby our thoughts are neither in the past nor in the future. During this meditation, we are filling our minds with focused thoughts on two of our senses; what we are hearing and what we are feeling touch our body.

As I mentioned in the previous chapter, these senses are very important to our state of being. They operate twenty-four seven whereas the sense of sight, smell and taste are transient to external stimuli.

By focusing our mind on what we are experiencing through sounds and touch, we automatically begin to release the thoughts that we began with before meditation. As a consequence, our physical body will automatically begin to relax.

Although this meditation can be done anywhere, I recommend that you begin by setting up a special place in your home. Many people consider these areas to be small shrines or altars where they can meditate and pray on a regular basis. This sacred space helps one feel connected to the divine world whenever they even look at it!

In your sacred space, place objects that help you feel a spiritual connection and are conducive to relaxation. Common items are crosses, crystals, rosaries, statues of angels, feathers, special rocks, etc. Most people relax better with a lit candle, so if you have one available, add this to your area.

It's best to leave this area set up (except for the lit candle) but not super critical. The reasoning behind this is if we make it too complicated by having to gather too much "stuff" each time we want to meditate, we will discourage ourselves from the session.

Another reason is that we will naturally start to relax when we go to this area because of conditioning. Our brain establishes a neural pathway or a memory that includes what we are experiencing through all of our five senses. As we begin to experience a relaxed state while in our sacred space, our brain stores the information. Upon further visits to your space, your brain retrieves the memory/experience and begins to send the relaxation signals before you even begin to meditate. It is actually more complicated than this but I thought I would just share a tidbit about it.

What my angels want me to point out here, is how incredible our brain is. The above example is a response that is based on our five senses without a conscious thought but the brain is capable of so much more. With a focused thought, we can establish new neural pathways that benefit us.

I know I'm getting off topic a bit, but I'd like to share a little about developing a new neural pathway regarding undesirable thought processes. There are many people who focus their thoughts on negativity and most of this is a learned behavior. Although some think that this habit cannot be changed as we age, I can assure you that this is not true. Yes, old dogs can learn new tricks.

The way to do this is to condition ourselves by focusing our thoughts on positivity. In the beginning, it requires effort as it is not what we are used to doing. After a certain amount of time, it becomes the new norm and much easier.

A simple analogy would be to imagine a worn pathway that represents negative thought processes. Since this pathway is no longer serving your highest good, it is time to establish a new path. As you focus your thoughts differently, a new pathway develops that eventually automatically becomes the one of choice. The old pathway is still there, but becomes overgrown with disuse.

Another analogy pertains to a routine, such as driving home from work. Most of us have experienced a phenomenon where we felt like we were on autopilot. We didn't have to focus our thoughts on getting home as there was a very solid neural pathway (memory) embedded in our brain.

If we had to take a different route home, we would have to focus our thoughts on the new route. This would create a new neural pathway in the brain. The longer that we travel this route, the better we remember it. Eventually, we can travel this route with ease and not have to think so hard about it.

Well, let's get back to the meditation stuff . . .

Although music can also help facilitate a spiritual connection during meditation, I would recommend beginning without it. It doesn't need to be perfectly quiet as some sounds are desirable with this type of meditation. The purpose here is to practice paying attention to the ambient sounds around you and music would interfere with that.

After you have a full grasp on the concept of mindfulness meditation, I would suggest then adding music for an additional benefit. There are some amazing songs and instrumentals available that are quite conducive for relaxation. There is also music easily available that can assist one in reaching a higher level of spiritual enlightenment.

As you find these types of music, just remember to not be afraid. There are many that are fearful of chants and music from other countries, but rest assured that they cannot harm you.

With that being said, we will now practice a general meditation.

1. Begin by getting in a comfortable position. Look at the special items that you have set out for yourself, enjoying the beauty of each and every one. Think about your spiritual self and what you want to achieve during this session. Say a short prayer of your choosing and ask for a divine connection to occur during your meditation.

2. Now, close your eyes and allow all thoughts of the day's events, problems, issues, etc. to enter your mind. Yes, I said "enter your mind". Recognize them but do not dwell on any one thought. Imagine that they are entering one ear and allow them to exit through the opposite ear. You are acknowledging your own thought process. If you are experiencing a recurring thought or worry, simply write it down so you can deal with it after your meditation session.

3. If you feel it helps, you can now say out loud or in your head "Egobegone" a few times to help release your logical thought process and making way for divine communication. Again, it can be pronounced exactly as it is spelled and is simply a consolidation of three words "ego", "be", and "gone". If you add an additional syllable on the end, this may be your angels helping with the cadence so just go with it!

With practice, you will be able to leave your eyes open and achieve a relaxed state but beginners should close them. The visual stimulation can be distracting until you have learned how to tune it out.

4. Next, begin to pay attention to your surroundings with your ears. Listen to all of the sounds within your room. As you focus on your listening skill, thoughts of the day's events will get fewer and fewer. You may hear quiet or loud sounds within the room from the air conditioner, refrigerator, ceiling fan, window unit or normal creaking noises that some homes make. Don't allow them to bother you, just listen. If it's very quiet, you can also listen to the sound of your own breathing or any movements that you make. It is not necessary to be completely still and if you are uncomfortable, simply reposition yourself.

5. Also, pay attention to the sounds that may be coming from outside your home. Listen for the quiet chirping of birds or crickets, the slight rumble of a distant airplane, the carefree innocent sounds of children playing, the low humming of a lawn mower, or the various sounds associated with nearby traffic, etc. Also, listen for any weather related sounds such as the wind blowing, the slight rumbling of thunder or the light pitter-patter of a gentle rain. You should be starting to relax already.

6. Now, shift your thoughts to your sensation of touch. Focus on how the air feels against your skin and whether there is any movement of it from a fan, etc. Describe to yourself how the atmosphere in the room feels. Is the room warm and comfy? Cool and relaxing? Damp or dry?

   Be careful about what words you use as descriptors. A warm room with a high humidity level could be described as "hot and muggy" or "warm and damp". The first description creates a feeling of being uncomfortable whereas the second one is a more neutral description.

7. Now, think about how your feet feel inside your shoes or against the floor and describe to yourself what it feels like. Is it soft, firm, warm, cold, fuzzy,

cushiony? Here again, choose descriptors that are conducive to positive thoughts rather than negative thoughts.

For example, the floor may be hard and cold but describe it to yourself as firm and cool. Your brain will perceive these words as powerful and strong rather than weak and detached. You are now relaxing and creating positive brain chemicals!

8. Toggle back and forth between each sensation for a bit until you are no longer thinking about the day's events and you are relaxed. If this is not happening, add additional pleasant descriptors and repeat the above exercise or continue on to the next step.

9. Now, shift your focus to your "mind's eye" which can "see" visual images with the eyes open or closed. At first you will feel like you are looking at the back of your eyelid and this is normal. If there is light in the room, it may appear dark reddish brown. If you are outside in the daylight, it will be brighter and you may also see any floaters that you have. What you see will change as your thought process moves into the next step which is visualization.

Eye floaters appear as small dots or squiggly lines that move as you try to focus on them. They are very

*common in adults and don't normally interfere with
vision.*

*As a reminder, the "mind's eye" is a term associated
with our brain's ability to visualize something. It is
closely associated with our memory and imagination
but can also be influenced by a supernatural source,
such as your angels. The mind's eye images can be
in color or black and white; and can be in the form
of movies, slides or snapshots.*

10. Next, focus your mind's eye on seeing a pleasant
    outdoor spot that you have visited or have seen a
    picture of. It could be on the beach, on a hilltop, at
    the lake or any spot that you felt a connection to for
    relaxation.

11. In your mind's eye, look around the area and enjoy
    the beauty. Study the details and describe them to
    yourself. Use words that create positive feelings
    about the experience. Always end the description
    with a positive affirmation.

Example 1:

*A beach description might be "I am sitting
comfortably at a warm sunny beach with soft golden
sand. The amazing blue sky is filled with white*

puffy clouds and I can feel the warm breeze blowing gently through my hair. I am at peace."

<u>*Example 2:*</u>

A hilltop description might be "I am sitting comfortably on a warm flat rock overlooking a beautiful green valley. I can hear the melody of spring through the occasional soft chirping of tiny innocent birds. I am serene and one with the universe."

<u>*Example 3:*</u>

A lakeside description might be "I am sitting comfortably on a velvety green lawn overlooking a lake filled with tranquility. I can hear a gentle breeze work its way through the majestic pines as if calling my name. My heart is filled with joy."

12. As you look around your "happy place" focus your thoughts on how you feel. By now, you should be calm and relaxed. You may experience an overwhelming feeling that you need to cry and this is normal. If this happens, do not hold back but simply let the tears flow.

    Crying can be very healthy in releasing pent up emotion or it can be a result of pure joy! Just remember to concentrate your thoughts on all things happy during the release. You are safe. You are special. You are loved.

13. If you are not in a calm and relaxed state, switch your thoughts back to your physical surroundings. Focus your thoughts on the ambient sounds in the room and the sensations that your body feels.

14. Continue this meditation for as long as you like. Since it is not a deep meditation, you can simply open your eyes or you can visualize yourself standing up, stretching your body and leaving your "happy place", knowing that you can return at any time.

If you continue to have difficulty, try adding soft relaxing music to this exercise. If this still doesn't work, just try again another day!

The goal of this meditation is to just simply relax. If your mind wanders off to a different location, don't try to redirect it back to your original imagery. This may be where the angels want your visualization to occur and they know best!

There may also be times when the place you start at begins to morph into something more ethereal. I had this type of experience where the visual images began to look similar to a kaleidoscope and then changed into a star filled galaxy.

If this happens, just enjoy the scenery as you are probably being guided by your angels to have a truly supernatural and sometimes out-of-body like experience for your enjoyment!

If there is anything unusual about your surroundings during this meditation, your angels may already be sending you information. You may see other people being present within your scene or events taking place. Here again, the angels may show it to you in the form of a movie or it may be in still pictures. Seeing a lot of detail usually indicates external information.

Mindfulness meditation can be practiced in any environment and is an easy way to relax, experience divine communication (next chapter!) or to relieve anxiety. I once taught this technique to a young girl at a noisy bar who was prone to anxiety.

I began by instructing her to close her eyes and pay attention to the sound of my voice and the other sounds within the room. I then asked her to focus her thoughts on how the floor felt beneath her feet, quickly describing the vibration underneath us. Within about 15 seconds, she opened her eyes and happily looked at me but a little puzzled. She had immediately relaxed with this simple technique!

Next, we are going to learn how to use meditation plus a few other techniques to connect with our angels!

Chapter Six

Connecting With Intention

I decided to break out the connection chapters as I realized that there are really two ways to communicate with the divine world. The first one is an intentional connection whereby one exerts an effort to receive information. This can be achieved through meditation, automatic writing, stream of thought sessions, simple requests and by using angel connection tools.

The other one is where the information just comes through without us requesting it. This is considered connecting without intention. This would cover dreaming; daydreaming; signs; and channeling through speech and body movement. As you become more experienced with your angelic connection, these methods can operate continuously. The angels would still like you to practice the intentional communicating, though, as there is great benefit in this as well.

Let's go over each area in detail:

Meditation

Begin a general meditation by completing steps 1 through 8 as outlined in Chapter 5, then continue as follows:

1. Instead of visualizing a "happy place" in your mind's eye, picture what your front door looks like (we talked about this in an earlier chapter). Examine it closely, paying attention to all the details of the door. What color is it? Is it steel or wood? Where is the door knob or handle located? Does it have windows?

2. Now, in your mind's eye, open the door and walk into your home. Look around the room, noticing where all of the furniture is located, what pictures or other decorations are on the walls and any other décor that comes to your mind. Pay close attention to all of the details. What you are seeing is based on memory.

3. Continue to walk through your home and enter your living area or another room of your choosing. Here again, pay attention to everything in the room, including the details about curtains, windows, rugs, etc. Notice the colors, shapes, textures and any other characteristics of the room. If you are like me, you will even notice what furniture needs dusting! While in this room, imagine that there is a birthday

party going on. Look around and notice the people, balloons and even the cake. Since I have made this suggestion to you, this visualization is now based on memory and imagination.

4. Now, imagine that everyone has left the party and everything has been cleaned up. Look around the room again and see if there is anything that doesn't seem to belong. An example would be if you "see" a pink elephant in your living room. Seeing an elephant would not logically be anything that you would retrieve from your memory or conjure up in your imagination.

   Visualization is closely associated with our memory and imagination but can also be influenced by external sources, such as our angels. In the beginning, the angels will insert images that do not logically go with your scene. The reasoning behind this as most people would discount anything that "logically fits" as their own imagination. Anything that doesn't "logically fit" would be considered external information.

5. Continue to look around to see if there is anything else of interest. Here again, if your mind wanders off to a different location, just allow it to do so.

6. If you arrive at a different location, just continue this exercise and notice if there is anything in your visual imagery that doesn't look like it belongs.

Example: As you walk through your home, it begins to disappear and you find yourself sitting at the beach. At first glance, everything seems to be normal and nothing is out of the ordinary. As you look out into the sky, you see a bird flying in the distance. As it gets closer, you recognize it as a giant bird. When it gets close enough for you to make out the details, you notice that it is a giant prehistoric flying dinosaur known as a pterodactyl.

This was my own personal experience which I knew was not my own imagination because I am not interested in dinosaurs. If it had been a UFO, I might have considered it my imagination as this is a subject that I am interested in. Angels will usually insert images that are far removed from what our personal imagination would come up with.

Again, the purpose of this is for us to recognize the information as being external to our own thought process. It can sometimes be relevant to our lives but not always. Be sure and don't place too much importance on the information as the angels will always repeat the messages that we most need to

receive. In other words, don't overanalyze and cause
yourself distress.

7. Continue this meditation until you feel like there
   is no more information being sent. Since it is not
   a deep meditation, you can simply open your eyes
   or you can go back to the front door, exiting your
   home. If you do this, don't forget to close the door
   behind you!

If you "see" someone with you during your meditation,
just acknowledge their presence and they may respond.
The angels will frequently allow our loved ones or
other departed souls to communicate with us during
meditation or even during a non-meditative state. They
may respond to you with a nod, a wink, a wave or may
give you a thumbs up signal. They may also blow you
a kiss or send a personal message that only you will
understand.

Practice is a big part of confidence building in knowing
that you are in communication with an ethereal being or
a loved one. In time, you will build up your confidence
as to the origin of the images and begin to trust that
the information is accurate. At some point, the imagery
that you receive will be logical but you will trust the
source as external.

Example: As I walked through my home during meditation, I gravitated towards the kitchen. In my mind's eye, I saw a pie sitting on the counter. I noticed that it had a lattice type crust on the top and had a dark berry filling. I felt like it was a blackberry pie.

Visualizing a pie in the kitchen makes sense and most beginners would discount this information as their own imagination. I knew that it was not for a variety of reasons. I don't bake pies and I don't like blackberries as they get caught in my teeth. I realize now that I experienced this visualization as an additional step for instruction.

Angels can send us all kinds of information for practice, but I'd like to share a bit more on how they worked with me. I feel like many of you will have the same or similar type experiences. I call this technique their "flash card" method. Yes, in a lot of ways, we are just children, learning a new skill.

I was in a light meditative state when I saw an image of an orange. I discounted the image at first but then it changed into an apple. Then, the apple changed into a banana. I thought this was my imagination as the images were all a part of a series. They were images of simple fruit pictures with basic colors.

The images continued with fruits that I was familiar with such as green grapes and kiwi. Then, something interesting happened. I saw an image of a piece of fruit that I couldn't immediately remember the name of. As my brain was searching for the word, "pomegranate", the image changed into a different piece of fruit.

I could not recall the name of that piece of fruit at all. Again, my mind was focused on trying to remember what it was called, when another image appeared. Then, they began to change again as if someone was showing me a rapid succession of flash cards.

I guess I was still not convinced that this was external information, so my angels switched it up a bit. I began to see, in my mind's eye, iconic images. I believe the first one was the Eiffel Tower. Then those, too, began to switch in rapid succession. I saw images of the Sphinx, the London Bridge, the Pyramids and even the Astrodome in Houston, Texas! This last image is in my neck of the woods which tells me that these images could be strictly personal to the viewer.

And, if that isn't cool enough, the images changed again and I could now clearly see cartoon characters that I was familiar with! At this point, I didn't even try to mentally identify them. I simply watched the series of pictures that they sent me. I remember laughing to myself and enjoying the experience. This was a wonderful lesson to teach me how to trust my mind's eye images! And, now I can pass this along to you just in case you should receive the same type of information!

Once your confidence improves that you are truly in connection, you will trust the information that is being sent. Keep in mind that not all information involves major stuff. Sometimes, it is to simply help our daily lives run smoother so that we are happier.

Practical application of this skill set can help you in a multitude of ways. The angels can send visual images to help us remember simple stuff like birthdays and appointments or to even find lost items. They can also send us images that help us prepare for our day, such as "seeing" an umbrella in our mind's eye.

Keep in mind that sometimes this information is not going to be direct. In other words, if you should see an umbrella and it doesn't rain that day, don't be discouraged. It might take a few days or weeks before you will understand what it meant. Pay attention to any kind of connection that happens.

An example would be to receive the image of an umbrella but it doesn't rain. You forget to take it back in the house and the following weekend, you attend an outdoor event and it provides the shade that you need.

Automatic Writing

Automatic writing is considered to be the process of putting words on paper without conscious thought or intent. It is believed to come from either the subconscious or a supernatural source.

Although there are folks who can do this either through pen and paper or through a computer keyboard, most folks will probably not be completely capable in the beginning. The reasoning behind this is the angels do not want us to be alarmed and many would get frightened by their hand moving independent of their thoughts. With that being said, the less fearful you are of the process, the more likely that you will be able to do this!

For the sake of this exercise, I will teach a form of automatic writing that my angels have taught me to get you started. In essence, it is partial automatic writing which involves your own thought processes along with channeled information.

Ready? Let's begin . . .

1. I recommend sitting at a table and placing a few objects around you that are of a spiritual nature. This will help you to have an optimal experience. Be sure and have a pen or pencil ready and some paper to write on.

2. First, write down the date and even the time, if you feel inclined to do so. Reviewing your sessions by date will help you measure your progress. Also, remember that numbers can frequently be a part of the information that is being sent.

3. Then, write down a few questions that you would like the divine world to answer. They can be specific or very general in nature. You can also address these questions to a being of your choice or just wait to see who comes through.

4. Close your eyes and briefly go through some of the meditative steps that we discussed in the previous chapter to assist you in relaxing and getting "out of your head".

5. When you are finished with your brief meditation, open your eyes and read the first question.

6. Write down the first thoughts or impressions that "pop" into your head as an answer to the question.

It does not need to make sense or even seem to be related to the question. It may sound silly or nonsensical, but this is okay. You will probably feel like you are having a conversation with yourself and this is normal. Just remember not to judge or filter your responses!

7. You may also think of musical lyrics, so make sure that you write this information down as well. The angels may be sending you a solution to a problem, a reminder about something that you have forgotten about or anything else that will be beneficial to you.

8. If you feel like drawing a picture or doodling, then do so as this can also be important.

Sometimes the angels or other divine beings will send information through the mind's eye in the way of basic or even abstract objects. My personal experience with this was during my very first communication effort a few years before my healing.

I "saw" what looked like building blocks in my mind's eye so I drew a picture of them. I also "saw" spirals so I wrote this down as well.

I was not clairaudient at the time and did not realize that I was actually in communication. I discovered this a few years later after I found my notes and looked at the date.

In retrospect, I realized that the blocks had significance in a couple of ways. It may have been a spiritual block that they were talking about as well as a physical block. I was later diagnosed with a rare muscle disorder that was created by a metabolic block.

For me, the spirals were also significant as they looked like strands of DNA. I believe my disorder was genetic and uncovering these old notes helped to reinforce my theory.

9. Continue your question and answer session for as long as you like or until you feel like you are not receiving any more information.

When you are finished, go back and read what was written. Pay attention to anything that seems odd to you. Angels frequently use several methods so that you will recognize the information as being external to your own thoughts.

Repetition is one of these means of identification. Look to see if you wrote anything down in multiples. People don't normally think in repetition. For example, if you asked a "yes or no" question and the answer you wrote down is "yes, yes, yes" then trust the information as external.

Here is an excerpt from my first book, *"Angel Talk"*, showing the significance of repetition.

"Eventually, I decided to try my hand at automatic writing. I was thinking that my hand would take off and move automatically but it did not. As a side note, this does happen for those who are not fearful of the divine process. I have since had a few experiences that were pretty amazing! I first wrote down a few questions that were on my mind. After each one, I began to write whatever thoughts popped into my head. At first I thought that I was just making up responses that I wanted to hear. Was this divine information or simply my imagination?"

"After I was healed, though, I reviewed all of my notes from that day. It seems that I was not only in communication with angels, but I had connected with my mother! There were many relevant responses to my questions from all of them, but there is one in particular that I would like to share with you. I wrote down the following question for my angels: 'Will I be healed?' The next few words would reveal their answer and my future."

"'In due time . . . in due time.'"

Angel Talk, Ch. 4 "Other Methods of Healing", p. 71

In the above example, you can see that I repeated "in due time" twice. The repetition is a hallmark of angelic communication but I did not know this at the time.

Unusual words or phrasing is another method that angels use to help us understand that we are in communication. If you use a word that is not normally a part of your vocabulary, then trust it to be external.

An example would be to use the word "forest" when you normally use the word "trees". Another good example is in the previous quote, when I wrote down "in due time" instead of a simple "yes".

Also, be sure and don't correct any misspellings. Many times these supposed errors involve a channeled communication!

Another way that angels help us understand their methods is by inserting endearments within our writing. If you are writing a response to a question, and you insert "dear", "sweetie", "love", etc., rest assured that the information is external!

I may be wrong, but I don't think they usually use "honey" as an endearment because it can have a strong association with sarcasm and as being derogatory. Although, if you have a deceased loved one who used this endearment, then it may very well be them that is communicating with you.

On a side note, angels always encourage us to give up sarcasm in our words and thoughts. Many people use sarcasm and believe it to be humorous. In most cases, it is just a venting of hostility under the guise of humor.

Sarcasm can be considered to be a passive-aggressive way of insulting someone else and that is always hurtful. Actually, the word, sarcasm has Greek origins and means "to tear or strip the flesh off". Now you know why you feel pain when you are at the receiving end of a sarcastic comment.

Sarcasm is also a way of feeding the ego part of our mind when we feel inadequate. There are many who use sarcasm to insult others so that they feel more important. In all reality, many of these same folks have real confidence issues.

The angels recommend that if we truly want to elevate spiritually, we will need to give up all negative words and thoughts and treat others with compassion and kindness. They are always most happy to assist us in this process!

There are also other ways in seeing divine communication during an automatic writing session. Writing down your own name is indicative of angelic communication. An example would be if I asked the question "Are my angels with me today?" and the response that I write down is "Cathy, yes they are always with you."

I might discount the information as external because the answer doesn't seem that odd. But, the information is certainly external in origin as I would not address myself by name on paper during an automatic writing session.

Nicknames that we have been known by can also be used by the angels. If your name is "Michael" and you write down an old nickname, "Mikey", during your session, then rest assured that there is divine communication happening! Also, if this was a pet name that a parent or other loved one used, then it could very well be them communicating with you.

The content of the response can help you identify who you are "talking" to. During my first automatic writing session, I drew a picture that had significance to my mother so I knew that she was "talking" to me during the session.

If you need clarification, just simply ask and respond with the answer that first "pops" into your head. It is always best to trust your gut feeling about who is present.

Also, look for anything that appears to be playful or sing-song within your writing. Angels want you to have fun with this process and frequently insert lighthearted and humorous messages. They know exactly what will make you smile so the humor will be designed just for you!

I believe that the reasoning behind the humor within these sessions serves an important purpose. Many people want to ask the angels to help them connect with departed loved ones which can be very emotionally painful. Humor helps alleviate some of this pain and can help our hearts heal.

Stream of Thought

Stream of thought (or stream of consciousness) is a process whereby you allow your thoughts to flow freely without inhibition or interference by logic and reasoning. It is influenced by the information that you have learned through your life experiences but can be heavily influenced by the divine world. It is a little different than "train of thought" as this method of thinking is based on logical processing.

In some respects, this exercise is very similar to automatic writing. Although stream of thought can involve feelings, images and ideas as well, it is simpler to begin this exercise with one word to understand the process. I have nicknamed this particular exercise the "Word Game".

1. I recommend sitting at a table and placing a few objects around you that are of a spiritual nature. Be sure and have a pen or pencil ready and some paper to write on.

2. First, write down the date and even the time, if you feel inclined to do so. Numbers can frequently be a part of the information that is being sent.

3. Close your eyes and briefly go through some of the meditative steps that we discussed in the previous chapter to assist you in relaxing and getting "out of your head".

4. When you are finished with your brief meditation, open your eyes and write down one word. It doesn't matter what the word is.

5. Next, write down the first word or words that "pop" into your head. It does not need to make sense or even seem to be related to the previous word, just

whatever you think of next. The first example is from a personal experience.

Example 1: I wrote down the word bird, then followed with birdbath; fountain; fountain of youth; youth dew perfume. I immediately thought about my grandmother who wore this perfume and assumed that she was making a connection with me.

Example 2: word, book, airfare, vacation, beach, sunny, skies, relax, enjoy, rejuvenate. In this example, notice that the "stream of thought" is now focused on a vacation. This may very well be your angels suggested that you take some time off to relax and enjoy life!

Example 3: music, country, rock, rockabilly, rock-a-bye-baby.

Now, you will probably stop and ponder whether this message is about someone named Billy, Bill or William or whether there is a new baby nearby for you or someone else. Ask your angels for clarification and continue.

Billy or baby? Baby, babycakes, pitter-patter of little feet, something very good to eat, watch your weight and avoid the treat.

In this example, a single word has evolved into a cohesive string of words and is sing-song and somewhat humorous. There are several different interpretations to this and many times, they will overlap. The angels may be informing you of an upcoming pregnancy of your own or for someone around you. There may also be someone in the picture with the name William, Billy or Bill. You also may be receiving a message to watch your diet and avoid sweets.

I noticed that within the example above several peculiarities that indicated an external source of information. A few of the words that I wrote are not a normal part of my vocabulary. I don't often use the words "rockabilly" or "babycakes" so I knew that they were external to my normal thought process.

Because I like to research, I would normally look up those words on the internet. There is sometimes useful information on the web that the angels can lead us right into! Also, pay attention to those little ads, etc. that you once thought were annoying!

I also noticed the sing-song and rhyming pattern to my wording that was very basic. This type of response is typical of angelic communication as it is lighthearted and fun.

I could go on and on with examples as I love practicing this exercise in obtaining information for myself or for others (and I'm thinking that this is a real message for someone). Now, let's finish up this exercise . . .

6. If you feel like drawing a picture or doodling during this exercise, then do so as it could be important.

7. Continue this session for as long as you like or until you feel that you are no longer receiving information.

Practicing stream of thought exercises using words is a fun and useful way to receive information from your angels or other divine beings! After you understand the process, begin with a string of words or an idea and see where that leads you!

Simple Requests

Simple requests involve asking a question and receiving an immediate response. The request can be said aloud or it can be a telepathic request. A telepathic request is simply asking an angel a question in your head.

Example 1: You have misplaced a ring that has sentimental value to you. You retrace your steps to see where it could be and cannot find it. You politely ask your angels where it is. The location suddenly "pops" into your head in either a visual image (clairvoyance) or just a sense of knowing (claircognizance). This means that you have just received divine information!

This is an example of an experience whereby you received knowledge that you could not have known. Although this manner is very direct, there are a multitude of ways that the angels can help in this situation.

Scenario 1: While looking for the ring, you suddenly remember that there is an important receipt in your pocket that you don't want to lose. While looking for the receipt, you find the lost ring.

Scenario 2: While looking for the ring, you find yourself thinking about the nursery rhyme, "Mary, Mary, quite contrary". Puzzled, you finish the lyrics out "How does your garden grow?" and suddenly remember that you had not checked the garden where you had been working earlier that day. Upon closer inspection, you find the ring sitting on the bench outside near the garden.

It's important not to discount thoughts that appear to be random and not connected to what you have asked for. Angels are very creative in the manner that they communicate information to us. Many times, the information also has other purposes.

In the above example, as you find the ring, you may notice that your prized flowers need watering or you have left the garden hose on. Just remember that angels take great care in making sure that our lives run as smoothly as possible!

<u>Example 2</u>: You are very tired but need to stop at the grocery store to pick up a few items. You ask your angels to help you find a close spot. You see a parking place that answers your request, but you inadvertently get delayed by another vehicle. Frustrated, you drive down the next row. You then remind yourself that you are healthy enough to walk and that the frustration is not good for you. After releasing this unhealthy emotion, you find another spot in front of you that is even closer!

The angels would like me to point out that it's important to be patient and not get upset when we feel that our requests are not being answered. In the above example, there may have been an additional "test" of patience and trust.

Also, there will be times that we are not going to receive the information that we ask for. Sometimes the angels are not allowed to deliver the answers to us. This means that it is either purposeful or it is not that important. When you are feeling frustrated, remember what I just wrote.

"It is purposeful" or "It is not that important."

There will be many times throughout our lives when unanswered requests are important in assuring a happy and successful life. The angels know what is in our future and always have our best interests in mind. ALWAYS.

Angel Connection Tools

Common angel connection tools include oracle cards, tarot cards and crystals but are not limited to these. A connection tool is simply an instrument that assists us in facilitating and understanding the messages that are being delivered.

There are many who are using these tools with great success but I have placed this information near the end of this chapter for a reason. My angels would like us to first learn how to meditate to get our connection since the world around us is so filled with noise. The meditation is extremely important to our overall well being.

They would also like us to learn how to communicate with them without using any tools. Always remember that the connection is not dependent on having a specific type of card deck or a particular kind of crystal. There are some who may not have access to any of these tools

83

and should be reassured that their intent will work just fine.

With all of that being said, the cards provide a beautiful and informative way to receive information from the angelic realm. It doesn't matter whether the cards are tarot or oracle cards as both will work.

From my understanding, the main difference is that angel tarot cards have a different format than the oracle cards. Tarot cards, in general, have been around for a long time and have historically had pictures that were quite frightening on them. Angel tarot cards follow the same format, but with attractive pictures and loving messages on them.

The angels would like me to let you know that even tarot cards with frightening pictures (skeletons, grim reaper, etc.) are not evil by themselves. It is the intention of the human using the cards that is important. Personally, I would not recommend them as many find the images disturbing and the pictures alone can create anxiety for the reader and any potential clients. Just remember that divine communication is about receiving and delivering loving messages!

Crystals can also be considered another connection tool and many use these to help facilitate their connection.

Although crystals can have very real energies about them, they are not necessary to communicate with the divine world.

One of the big purposes that they serve, though, is in creating an atmosphere conducive to spiritual connection. This visual atmosphere is a trigger for us to feel the connection and thus boosts our faith. Many crystals (as well as rocks) have associations to the angelic realm that people find desirable. If you'd like to use a crystal or a rock, I suggest that you find one that you like and feel a personal bond to.

Just remember, that in developing angelic communication, it is important to take time daily to work on your skills. Trust, practice, then put it all together. Your angels are there waiting for you to put forth your effort and will be glad to deliver information that you need. As I mentioned before "greater effort equals greater reward".

Chapter Seven

Connecting Without Intention

The second method of connection to the divine world is of the unintentional kind. Basically, this means that the information just comes through, even without your focused intention or effort. This covers dreaming, daydreaming, signs, channeling through speech and body movement.

Let's go over each area in detail:

Dreaming

Although the purpose of dreaming has been a controversial subject, we do know one thing. Everyone dreams. Many say that they don't dream but this is simply not true. They just can't recall their thoughts/dreams during sleep. With a little practice, even these people will be able to recall part of what they have dreamt.

My first recommendation if you are having difficulty remembering your dreams is to place a pen and paper beside the bed. Upon awakening, write down what you were thinking about or any part of a dream that you may remember at that time.

With a little practice, you will be able to recall many details about your dream. Most of this information needs to be documented before you begin your daily activity as it can soon be forgotten. Since much of it has no apparent meaning to us, we file away the memory into an "Other" folder. If it is important, though, our angels can help us find this file and retrieve a dream! By the way, this applies to memories, as well!

The meaning of our dreams is also a controversial subject and has been debated for years between psychologists and other researchers. The same dream can have a variety of interpretations, depending on who is doing the interpreting. I recommend that you don't get too caught up in any one interpretation and definitely don't worry about any of your dreams, regardless of the content. Worry is always a wasted emotion and definitely not in our best interest.

My angels have told me that some of our dreaming is just simply part of random brain activity. This activity can be generated from purposeful thoughts that we have had or subconscious thoughts. I won't get in to the technical stuff about the subconscious here as it is really not that important.

Dreaming can also be influenced by a variety of external sources. Some of these sources include smells, sounds, temperature, and internal body sensations. Have you ever dreamed about a bathroom/toilet and woke up, realizing that your bladder was full?

And, one other external source of influence is from the celestial realm. Angels can help us during our dream state find resolution to problems, help us with our creativity, connect us to departed loved ones, send futuristic information and even educate us!

It is fairly common for people to wake up with a sense of knowing how to resolve an issue or problem. Although some believe this information is generated by the subconscious mind, I feel like it is all divinely guided. If you have had this experience, reflect on whether there was anything unusual about your epiphany.

It is also common for people to wake up with new inspiration for projects or a desire to be creative. Angels help us during our sleep by sending the thoughts and ideas that they know will be useful in achieving our personal goals.

Angels will also help us connect with departed loved ones during our dream state. Many people report feeling like their loved one was truly present while they were dreaming. If you have experienced this, think back on how detailed the dream was. Although some dreams can be based from memory, the details and vividness of the dream help discern the origin.

Dreaming can also involve premonitions and precognitions sent from a divine source. Premonitions are generally considered to be feelings about something that has not happened yet, whereas precognitions are considered as having direct knowledge of the specific event.

It is common for many to use these words interchangeably but there is a slight difference in their meanings. While most equate premonitions with a negative connotation, it certainly does not always mean this. It is also not exclusive to the dream state and can happen even within waking hours.

Even though we can experience premonitions and precognitions in our waking state, they are more likely to appear in our dreams unless we engage in regular meditation. Sometimes it can be startling to see, read or experience something that has been previously dreamt about. Many times, though, this is just practice for us to get acquainted with a connection to the divine world.

In 2004, I dreamed about what I considered a tidal wave event. In the dream, I was at a tropical resort with palm trees, a beach and a mountainous hillside. I remember being inside of a car, looking in the rear view mirror and watching as a huge wave approached the shore. I remember being quite frightened and feeling like I had been engulfed by the water.

A few days later, I read in the newspaper about the Indian Ocean Earthquake and subsequent tsunami which took the lives of over 200,000 people. I now know that I was sent this information as a precognition of events to come. Although the dream was unpleasant, it showed me that I was capable of receiving "other worldly" information.

I believe that many people had the same type of dream. I'm not sure of the reason behind this but believe it has something to do with the major amount of energy that was released from the event. The earth experienced a huge physical shift and the heavenly world experienced a large number of new soul arrivals.

Both of these events create energy vibrations that can affect many people. Those vibrations begin to occur before the events happen and those who are intuitive can feel the effects of them. It is similar to animals behaving differently before a major weather or planetary event.

I also realize that the precognition of the tsunami was not meant for me to take action on. There was nothing I could do about it, except send out a prayer. There are other types of precognitions that might require some action, but my angels want me to explain a bit more about this.

Our angels want us to be safe and happy and not to worry about anything. I strongly feel that those who have requested daily assistance from the angelic realm should not be worried about missing the information in a precognition. Angels don't expect us to always understand this level of communication

With that in mind, they can alter our course if necessary without us having to deal with any anxiety about it. This means that if you receive a precognitive dream or a simple premonition about being in an automobile accident and subsequently forget about it, then your angels can divert your course, without you even knowing it.

If you do get involved in the accident (and then you remember the dream), then it's important to know that there was nothing that you could have done about it. I know this seems a little complicated, but the bottom line is to ask for protection, then release the worry and trust that you are divinely protected.

It is also important to remember that we should always live our lives in the manner that God intended for us. This means doing our best to be good people. Our actions and words should always be based on love. If not, we will be guided to make changes.

As a reminder, there will be times that people will have experiences where they feel that there was no protection. It is important to understand that sometimes there is a bigger reason for the experience to occur. What is important here is not to maintain focus on the negativity of a situation and to move forward with positive thoughts.

Also, there are times when it is simply our perception of the situation as negative. If you have experienced what you believed was a negative situation, think back to see if there was anything positive that came out of it. Was there a silver lining? Was there a lesson learned? Sometimes neither of these will seem to apply. It is at this point that we simply need to let go of the pain and any other negative thought processes surrounding it. These negative thought processes will only impede our spiritual progress.

Other types of precognitions that should be discussed here are those on a more positive note. Sometimes angels will send us information about our future. I have had several dreams about being interviewed on a stage by a talk show host about my miraculous healing and the angelic interaction. Although some could say this is wishful thinking, I feel quite sure that it will be in my future. If not, I have enjoyed "seeing" myself in the interview and knowing that my story is worthy of this type of publicity. It has also helped my confidence and that results in more dedication on my part to inspire others.

To finish up this section, I would also like to discuss what else can happen during our sleep. It is not uncommon for people to feel tired upon awakening and to feel like they were very busy while sleeping. Sometimes the angels will school us on a variety of topics during this time but will always make sure that we get enough rest. Many people refer to this schooling as "downloads" as there can be quite a bit of information sent to us during our sleep!

Although this information can be sent to us at any time, the angels like to relay it to us during our sleep. I believe that this is important as we don't have ego-minded thoughts interfering with the information. We don't try to discount it; we just accept it as is.

Another important reason is that when we are sleeping (or drifting off to sleep), we are less fearful. This is a particularly important point for those of you who are becoming clairaudient.

Hearing voices in the waking state, for many people, can be frightening and the angels know this. In order to avoid this fear, they speak to us while we are drifting off to sleep or just waking up. Most will discount these voices as being a part of a dream.

As we learn more about the gift of clairaudience, we understand the voices to be of a divine origin and are less afraid. When we finally release this fear, they are allowed to speak louder and plainer so we can receive the most information from them.

With this being said, though, timing is always important so be patient if you are working on becoming clairaudient. They will prepare you along the way for your particular journey. Many will experience tinnitus or other ringing and buzzing sounds for awhile before making the sounds out to be words.

Sometimes, the sounds will even sound like wind chimes or tinkling bells. As clairaudience progresses, you will feel like you are overhearing a conversation in the next room or listening to a radio or television station turned down quite low.

If you wish to work on this gift, ask your angels to help guide you into what you need. I believe that listening to white noise is important. It relaxes us and also allows us to recognize any sound or words that are outside the constant sound that is being produced.

As I mentioned in a previous chapter, listening to white noise also conditions the auditory nerve for the extra auditory stimulation of angelic communication. When I first became clairaudient, I sat by a fan in my bedroom so that I could hear them better.

So, whether you become clairaudient or not, it is important to know that a big part of your dreaming can be influenced from the divine world.

Daydreaming

Another way that angels communicate with us is through our daydreaming state. Most of us daydream when we are bored or tired and allow our minds to wander. Daydreaming is actually very close to being in a meditative state.

It is closely tied to fantasy and illusion and is a healthy way for our mind to escape from the day's events. We can lose total or partial awareness of our surroundings and reality can become quite blurry. Our minds wander off to a visualization that is enjoyable to us.

Angels can help "steer" our daydreams into information that we need to know or it can be merely for our enjoyment. Sometimes it is relevant to the present as in finding a solution to a problem. It can also be predictive in nature. Some daydreams allow us to see future events that may or may not impact us. This would be considered a wakeful precognition.

I have experienced a lot of inspiration (and hopefully precognitions) through what could be considered daydreaming while walking on my treadmill. There have been several times that I have visualized a movie that is based on my first book, *Angel Talk*.

I felt like I was daydreaming at times without any preconceived ideas of where the movie might go. At other times, though, I could steer the movie with my own thoughts. In some ways, this could be just visualization but it really doesn't matter. I believe the angels were sending me information through a daydream about a future movie that would be based on my book.

Based on that information, I decided that it would be a good idea to write a screenplay as another project! I'm not real sure where this project is going to fit in with my other ones, but I know that I will get perfect divine guidance on it!

Signs

Angels will also communicate with us through a variety of signs. The list could be endless so for simplicity I will share the most common ones, beginning with the visible ones.

Visible divine signs frequently include feathers, coins, butterflies, hummingbirds, dragonflies or any other winged creature or any animal. They also include billboards; street signs; any other written media that catches our attention; and repetitive or significant sequential numbers (more about this later).

The following two examples are from true events.

Example 1:

A friend of mine has a deceased family member (his mother) who was fond of hummingbirds. When he or other family members see one, they always think of her. On one occasion, a hummingbird flew very near his son's face and appeared to be looking at him before flying away.

Although, there is a logical association between their mother/grandmother and the hummingbird, there are details that reveal this to be divine. The unusual behavior of the bird combined with the son's first thought (his grandmother) indicates that this was indeed a divine encounter!

Other important signs to take note of in these types of experiences concern unusual timing of the event. Was this the appropriate time of the year to see hummingbirds? Did this occur on a significant date that was important to the deceased person? Be sure and recognize these unusual timing events before dismissing the experience as a coincidence.

Example 2:

While driving you notice the stop signs more than usual or you seem to always catch the red light. This could be a message for you to "stop" and pay attention to something that you are doing or could be a lesson in patience.

Example 3:

Although I was going to save this story for another book, I would like to share it here as well. This was a personal experience of mine that happened at my shop in Galveston, Texas.

"Bob and the Little White Feather"

One day at my shop in Galveston, I met a very nice man who was working in the Houston area. He traveled a lot with his job and actually lived out of state. He appeared to be a bit lonely and had been out strolling in the downtown Strand area when he "stumbled" into my shop.

I shared the story of my healing, including the information about me being clairaudient. I don't think he completely believed that I was in communication with the angelic realm, but I understood his skepticism. I felt a strong urge to suggest that he "slow down" a bit and watch for one of the angel's calling cards, which are feathers.

The next time I saw Bob, I was standing outside the front door of the shop and he exclaimed "Hey, I haven't seen any of those feathers, yet!" Well, at that very moment, a slight breeze kicked up and a single feather blew down the sidewalk right in front of us! I casually said something like "Well, there you go, there's your sign!" He chuckled a bit and I truly believe that he blew it off as coincidence, although I'm sure it gave him some enjoyment.

The next time I saw Bob, we were having a serious discussion at my front counter. Both of us were casually leaning on it with our elbows gently resting against the glass. We were again discussing the feather business and if my memory serves me correct, he mentioned that the incident was really neat. I again reassured him that these were indeed real signs of angelic presence and not simply coincidences.

At that precise moment, something caught my eye. Without turning my head, I noticed a very tiny white feather drifting over my right shoulder as if in slow motion! It was coming from the back of the shop which is directly opposite of my front door. It continued its leisurely path across my shoulder and gently landed on the front counter, directly between us! I looked up at him, knowing that he had seen the entire event and I softly said, "There's your sign."

Folks, this was impressive, even for me! I believe in my heart that Bob needed to see this incredible event to help convince him that there is a world out there that can help us if we ask. We have since discussed the incident and I noticed that he is happier and has quit smoking. I don't know if all of his problems have been solved, but he now has the vivid memory of the little white feather to remind him that "all things are possible".

I have since seen many a feather when I needed a sign but this particular incident still amazes me!

Another visible sign of angelic communication that I would like to address is about numbers. Repetitive numbers, (111, 222, 333, etc.) or any sequence of numbers seen repetitively (123, 123, 123, etc.) is probably angelic.

Repetition is a hallmark indication of their interaction. The human brain is wired so that patterns catch our attention and that is why our angels use them. They typically draw our attention to these repetitive numbers to give us information.

In general, it can simply be reassurance of their presence. The numbers can also have other meanings that may be personal to you. If you are seeing repetitive numbers, you can also look them up on various internet resources. I recommend that you always trust your gut on what you are reading to see if it applies to you.

Even though I can hear my angels audibly, I sometimes need extra signs such as the ones I just discussed. A few years back, my sister left the assisted living home she was at and was missing for several weeks. My angels reassured me that she was safe but I still worried about her.

I had requested my angels on several occasions to help me locate her but they were not allowed to do so. I remember being in a department store one day shopping and thinking about where she might be. At that moment, I reached down into my purse to check my phone and noticed that the time was 1:11.

It was then that I gave up the rest of my worries and trusted that all was as it should be. I knew within my heart that regardless of the outcome, it was going to be okay and there was nothing I could do to change it. The worry would only create distress for me and that is not what I needed or wanted.

There are other signs that concern numbers that are divinely sent. If a family member wishes to connect with you, the angels may help draw your attention to a number that is significant to them, such as a birth date, anniversary or transition date (the date they passed away).

Keep in mind that a visible sign should be interpreted with what your gut feeling is. It is this first impression (thoughts and feelings) that will determine what the sign means. This means that the interpretation may be individual to the recipient.

For example, one person may find a penny lying on the ground and feel a strong connection to their angels whereas another may think of a deceased loved one who collected pennies. Another may think about a friend who has the name "Penny" and feel a need to call.

In addition to these visible signs, angels can relay messages to us audibly. They can send these messages through the radio, television or even other people's conversations. They help us receive this information by helping our ears to "perk up" so that we can hear them even if we are not really paying attention.

This is one of the ways that our angels will convey what name that they would like for us to call them. The name can sound louder or we suddenly feel the need to listen carefully. I went over this a bit in Chapter One.

Hearing a significant song on the radio is one very common method of communication. Here recently I have awakened twice to a song that includes the lyrics "It's a beautiful day". What is unusual is that after I turned off the alarm I realized that I didn't hear any other part of the song. All I heard was "It's a beautiful day!" This example is what I would consider a "wonderment" type of message that is designed to simply brighten up our day!

Another example of communication through the radio recently occurred to my husband while he and I were traveling. After I sneezed, he heard a voice say "Gesundheit" over the radio. At first, he thought it was just a coincidence until he realized that it could not have been part of the radio conversation.

Gesundheit is the German word for health and is typically said after someone sneezes. It has personal significance for me as my father used to say this. He frequently spoke bits and pieces of German as this was his heritage and he was very proud of it!

I didn't immediately think about my dad when the incident occurred so I think it may have just been the angels working with my husband. Since he was the one that heard it, the message was probably designed for him, although I greatly enjoyed the experience, myself!

Channeling through Speech

Have you ever felt like you came up with just the right words for someone in need? Did you think to yourself "I don't know where that came from?" Perhaps, someone responded to you with "That is exactly what I needed to hear today!"

Angels can help us to assist others by channeling the words or wording that someone else needs to hear. They know exactly what will make a difference for the recipient of your good intentions. Many people have experienced this but did not realize that it was of divine origin.

The angels would like us to know that they are not going to put words in our mouth that we will be unhappy about. This process is not one to be feared but welcomed. As humans, our emotions sometimes get in the way and we can get flustered when trying to console or counsel someone. Another reason for them to channel through us is of even greater importance. There are many times that our words have a tremendous impact on others and they need to be chosen carefully. Sometimes the angels need to choose them for us.

A few years back, I had a profound experience concerning angelic channeling as well as divine timing. It was after this particular incident that I truly understood how important our wording can be and how important we are to each other. It also serves as confirmation of how divine synchronicity can work.

This experience began as a simple birthday celebration for one of our family members. We usually celebrated at a particular restaurant which is about forty-five minutes away from my home. This restaurant also has a closer location that we occasionally went to. My son-in-law, Jason, was in charge of the plan and he decided to switch to the closer location even though it was farther away for his father and elderly grandmother to drive to. This was one of many odd events that happened.

Jason also decided at some point to change the time. I know that this was important as several other things happened after that. My husband and son were together that evening and decided to go early or didn't get the message of the time change. Since the rest of the party was not there, they decided to sit at the bar and have a drink before dinner. The chairs that they sat on were right near the restaurant's party room which was not open that evening. We were very familiar with the room as that is where many of our gatherings had occurred.

I arrived about 15-20 minutes later and joined them at the bar. They were actively engaged in conversation with a woman who was sitting alone and having dinner at the bar. My husband and son are very friendly so this did not surprise me. I believe that my husband had told the woman that I had written a book, so I gave her one of my business cards.

After taking a look at my card, she said "You do readings?" I replied to her that I did, although I was a little hesitant as she was moderately intoxicated. She proclaimed "Well, I'd like a reading! Can you do one right now!" I hesitated again as she seemed a little belligerent and I knew that I would miss part of the party. I felt a strong urge to go ahead with the reading but I quickly realized how noisy the environment was.

I suggested that we go into the party room as it was quiet and I knew that the restaurant would not mind. She left her meal at the bar and we went into the room. After we sat down, she asked if it was okay to record the session and I agreed. As usual, I began the session with a short prayer.

She seemed a bit testy and defiant so I wondered what I had gotten myself into. At first, I wasn't sure that she believed in intuitives/psychics as she immediately asked me if I could read her mind. I didn't get annoyed and just replied that if it was important enough, the angels would allow me to do so.

She then specifically asked me to tell her what she was thinking. I looked directly at her and calmly responded "Don't do it." She again said "Can you tell what I am thinking?" I said yes and again replied with the words, "Don't do it."

It was at that point that I realized what was happening. I knew that this woman was contemplating suicide. She then began to tell me about her elaborate and rather gruesome plan to kill herself because of all the problems that she was having at home. She began to cry and told me that she felt like God had abandoned her.

At that point, I could feel a warmth come over my entire body and I calmly responded with "He has not abandoned you, my dear, but has sent an angel to be with you on this very day."

That is when I knew, without a shadow of a doubt, that I had just channeled a direct message from the heavens.

We talked a bit more and I made some suggestions to her about what would help her situation. I told her that she should not kill herself and may have asked her to agree to this. She seemed much better after our talk and went back to her dinner.

After she left the room, I felt like I was in a daze. As I began to come out of it, I realized what had just happened. I began to cry, realizing that I may have just been the instrument that kept this person alive. After I gathered my wits about me, I exited the private room and joined the birthday celebration.

It is important for us to know that there are events in this world that are not orchestrated by humans, but rather by a loving energy source with perfect timing. *You see, the suicide that this woman talked about was to happen that very evening right after she finished her dinner.*

Although this event was somewhat startling for me, there were many lessons that were learned. I gained a better understanding of how the divine world works. From a human standpoint, this event seems rather complex. Many people had to be involved for the appropriate timing to occur. I understand better now, that there is nothing too complicated for our angels to handle. Here again, my trust and faith increased as to the power of that world.

Another lesson that can be learned from this is about flexibility and perspective. Although the venue and time changed for the party, no one became annoyed, even if they were inconvenienced. There are many times that people get frustrated or angry about changes or delays that interfere with their plans. It is important to know that there is a source that knows more than us and that we should trust that source.

If you find yourself in a situation that is beyond your control, remember to trust that you are at the right place at the right time, no matter what. Your perspective of the situation should always be from a positive angle.

Body Movements

Angels can also maneuver a part of or even our complete body in order to get something accomplished. Most of the time, people don't even realize that it is happening as the angels don't want to frighten us. They also don't want us to think of ourselves as puppets because we are most certainly not.

There has to be an established connection with them and the actions have to be important. I don't mean important as in life-threatening, even though this can occur as well. It just means that it has to be significant for the recipient and the interference has to be approved.

Humans have been given free will to live their lives in the manner that they choose to do so. It is their choice to enlist the assistance of the divine world during their life. Most of these people will receive the help that they need unless there is a more important purpose for them to not receive it.

I might add here that any of the manipulations by the angelic realm would also fall under the umbrella of having the "holy spirit" move through you. They are a big part of that divine holy world that some even refer to as simply "Spirit". Many people refer to these manipulations as divine interventions.

There are also other beings that will work through individuals to assist them. Jesus and Mother Mary are the two that came to mind first as I am most familiar with them. The being that connects, though, really depends on the background and training of the individual as well as who they request assistance from. For the sake of simplicity, I am going to just focus on how the angels work with us.

Many times angels can help us by gently moving our head so that we can see something. Most of the time, we don't even feel the movement as it is very subtle. They may also help us to turn our body in a certain direction if it is necessary at the time.

In addition, they can help us feel "drawn" to something that needs our attention. This doesn't necessarily include a body movement, but involves a gut feeling. The best way to explain this is to feel a certain amount of compulsion to turn our eyes towards an object, event, etc. The feeling can sometimes be quite strong and at other times, almost go unnoticed. I have experienced feeling "drawn" to look at something in both manners but barely notice it now.

I think that as we get more comfortable with our angelic connection, all types of communication from them become more fluid with our daily lives. We also are not as afraid of the communication and don't resist or ignore the information. It simply becomes a way of life.

Many times, people are drawn to look at the clock at a certain time and will see repetitive numbers. This can also happen with license plates or anywhere that numbers can be found. These numbers may have a special meaning or may just be a sign of angelic presence. If you find this happening, you can feel quite confident that you are experiencing an angelic sign!

This also happens with other scenarios as well. Angels can gently guide you to look at anything that you need to see. In addition to numbers, they use this manner to help folks see anything that is significant for that individual. It can be as simple as finding a lost object or as complex as keeping an eye on young children.

In the previous chapter, I discussed automatic writing and how one could request messages through this manner. There are also other times, though, where the angels deliver the information through writing without our specifically requesting it. I know that while writing this book, there have been times that I begin to type words that I was not really intending on typing.

Currently, when they work with me, they do not completely take over the keyboard (or my pen), but simply guide my hands (as well as my thoughts) to a word or phrase that helps me type the information that needs to be delivered. It is all very fluid and for the most part, the information is in my personal tone of voice.

There are many times, though, that I can tell when they are speaking directly. The tone changes and becomes a bit more formal or my wording is a little different than usual. I can also identify their direct information by the fact that I will use words that are unusual to my normal jargon. I am hoping that in the near future that they will channel a book that is entirely of their words!

There are many other situations where the angels will become involved and work through other parts of our bodies. I have had a few of these experiences that I recognized as angelic intervention.

In my book, *Angel Talk*, I relayed a story about how my angels helped me with a foot injury. I was unable to rehabilitate it through my own exercises and after several months, an amazing, yet very simple event occurred. Here's an excerpt concerning this event . . .

"On another occasion, they helped me with an injury to my right foot. I hurt it just after I returned to play soccer. Yes, I did get to go back and play! I had only participated a few minutes when I took a simple misstep. I heard a popping noise and felt pain on the top of the foot. I had broken my right ankle several years earlier and wondered if the foot was a little weak. I was a little miffed again that my angels allowed me to hurt myself but wasn't too upset about it. There is always more to it than what meets the eye! Evidently, I had not done enough conditioning or the incident served another purpose.

After the injury, I tried for several months to rehabilitate my foot. I knew all of the appropriate exercises and stretches because of the broken ankle. I didn't feel like I was making much progress and I kept getting set back every time I tried to ramp up my walking efforts.

On one particular occasion, my angels guided me into an unusual stretch before walking. I took an unusual step backwards on the injured foot and put all of my weight on it. I bent my knee as if stretching my calf muscle and began lifting my heel up and down. I could feel the gentle stretching on the top of the foot and think there may have even been a few little popping sounds. I realized that this was *not a stretch that I came up with but one that they guided my physical body into doing. I now continue that same stretch and no longer have any problems with that foot!"*

Angel Talk, Ch. 9 "Family of Miracles", p. 191

On a different occasion, I was trying to put a box back up on the top shelf of a very crowded and awkward closet. As I was struggling, I could sense that my angels wanted me to ask for their help. I don't think that I heard it audibly.

At first, I declined as I thought it was too mundane of a request for them to help with. While I struggled, I felt like they were patiently looking over my shoulder waiting for me to get frustrated enough to request their assistance. Well, this happened fairly quickly as I didn't have much patience that day for an ornery box.

Before I could completely finish the thought process of my formal request, something very interesting happened. I raised my left hand and gently pushed aside the impediment on the shelf, which ended up being the flap of another box.

At first I was a little startled as I would have expected them to tell me audibly or show me in my "mind's eye" what the problem was. Then I got very excited. Although, they had worked through me before, it was during this incident that I completely realized what they could do. I finally understood that if it was important enough, my angels could work through my hands or even my entire body!

I know that this particular story would normally be categorized to fall in the previous chapter, "Connecting with Intention", but I feel that it is beneficial to include it here. Most of the time, we don't think about requesting the angels to work through our bodies, but they do so on a regular basis.

The example that I just shared served many purposes, the main one having to do with trust and fear. Immediately after this occurred I realized that they could drive my car if necessary or even intervene in someone else's malicious intentions towards me.

It was after my "box in the closet" incident that I let go of any residual fear about this world. I realized that I could trust my angels to keep me safe, provided that this is a part of my life path. After releasing this fear, I began to release the rest of my worries as well.

When something happens where I don't feel like they intervened, then I know that it was purposeful or not important. This is really the key to accepting what happens to us in life. With this understanding, we free ourselves from negative thought processes, such as fear and worry. This allows room for the love and happiness that our angels want us to experience.

Another story that involves physical angelic intervention happened while my son-in-law was driving. As he and my daughter were going through an intersection, she noticed another vehicle quickly approaching her side of the truck. She gasped as she saw the lights approaching and remembered seeing (in her mind's eye) a horrific accident and her own death. At that same time, my son-in-law felt his grip on the steering wheel change and his accelerator press down which helped them clear the intersection faster.

They both quickly realized that if this had not happened, the other vehicle would have broadsided them on the passenger side. I feel sure that the vision that my daughter received was important. I believe one of the reasons was to show the seriousness of the incident had the angels not intervened. This helped bolster her faith and now serves to help others with their own faith as the story is shared.

I am extremely grateful for the divine intervention of angels on that day and all of the other days that they have assisted my family.

With all of this in mind, though, I do realize that not everyone is spared from accidents and other misfortunes. I know in my heart that many of these people were good and very faithful people. As mentioned before, there are circumstances when an event is going to happen without divine intervention. This is most likely because there was a plan in place that could not be changed.

Since we do not know what our plan or life's mission is with any certainty, I encourage everyone to request divine help. I believe that if we do our best here on earth to spread love and light messages to others, we also increase the possibility of being allowed to be here longer, regardless of any predetermined plan.

Chapter Eight

Becoming an Angel Intuitive

Once you realize that you are actually in communication with angels, several things begin to happen. You may reflect back on how you got to this point and see the divine orchestration that directed you. You will most likely develop an even greater thirst for knowledge and search out more books, articles and classes for further learning.

You may also begin to wonder why you have been guided to learn about your gifts and what you are supposed to do with them. At this point, you may even become a little frustrated as to what direction you should take. This is when it is important to be patient and realize that the information will be revealed to you at the appropriate time.

I might add here that the first manner of business that the angels will help you with is in healing yourself. By doing this, you develop the knowledge and experience to help others as well. Be honest about any shortcomings that you need to work on and make a list if you feel the need to do so. I will go into their healing techniques better in my next book as it is too much to include here. As an overview, though, their main focus is in helping you gain healthy thought processes; healthy lifestyle habits and a healthy spiritual outlook.

There are times that we don't want to face the truth about ourselves but it is absolutely necessary to do so. Just remember that the angelic world knows everything about us. You cannot hide anything from them as it is already known. They are not here to judge or criticize us but to teach us how to heal. They offer unconditional love, acceptance and guidance.

The angels have told me that it is very important for us to be happy during our stay on earth. The communication with them assists us in feeling this happiness and this spreads to others by what I like to refer to as osmosis. By this, I mean that others see your happiness and positivity and it lifts them up. This positive vibration is what will heal the planet.

It is important to not feel pressured or in a rush about fine tuning your gifts or any messages that come through. If you are experiencing this, please understand that it is self imposed. The angels want us to relax and enjoy our journey. If you feel "stuck" in your spiritual progression, though, then spend additional time in meditation and practice the exercises from Chapter 4. It also might be a good idea to reflect on any negative thoughts and ideas that you may still be holding on to.

Communicating with angels helps our lives run smoother and is very beneficial in any occupation. Having this intuitive skill set can assist teachers in "knowing" which student needs extra attention; help police officers "know" when a situation is going to become dangerous; and help doctors "feel" when a patient needs further testing. Most people understand that gut feeling but don't completely understand where it comes from.

The intuitive gift is also beneficial in occupations that deal with environmental issues. Healing our planet is of utmost importance and many will be guided to become a part of this. This may be your calling if you feel the need to become more active in environmental concerns.

I am being guided to include a bit more here about this. Becoming more active doesn't always mean becoming an activist, although this can be a part of your mission. Just remember that an angel guided activist would always stay calm, be peaceful, offer solutions and always offer positive words. Anything other than this lowers the vibration and adds to the chaos in the world.

Becoming active in this area might involve working towards cleaner fuel solutions; producing inventions or patents for cleaner living; supporting organic farming; and the list goes on. Many folks have already begun working in these areas in some form or fashion. Even recycling old material into something new is helping to protect our planet!

Although using your angelic connection within mainstream occupations is a great idea, many people are going to feel the need to do more. These intuitives will feel a strong desire to set up their own practice in doing readings and healing work. If this interests you, then read on!

After you have stated your intention to become an angel intuitive/healer (either orally, written or just a thought), you will notice certain things happening. Articles that interest you will suddenly appear while surfing the internet or while at a bookstore. You may overhear conversations about healing work. You may even feel "drawn" to go into a metaphysical shop to learn more.

Many people that come into my shop in Galveston have had this experience. Some have relayed to me that they really didn't know why they "happened upon" my shop! One man in particular told me that he had been "drawn" to visit Galveston and realized why after visiting my shop. What was interesting is that he came all the way from Asia!

I might add here that stating your intention to become an angel intuitive/healer is mainly for your own benefit. The angels already know what is in your heart. You may even notice that there are things that seem to have been orchestrated long before you made your intentions clear. It is really more about how good we feel after making an important decision. It also gives us direction.

For clarification, angel intuitives are those with psychic or intuitive gifts who are in direct communication with the angelic world. They may or may not have other guides that assist them with information. They use these gifts to heal themselves and others. After establishing a connection with your angels, you can consider yourself an angel intuitive, although most consider this a title that is associated with a profession.

Giving an angel reading is considered one way to help someone heal so these intuitives are considered healers and many are considered lightworkers. As a healer, you will be delivering information that will impact your clients on a physical, emotional and spiritual level.

My angels would like me to address a few points that deal with angel intuitive and other certification programs.

There are a few sources that offer these certifications (as well as related fields) but it is not absolutely necessary to have them. The benefit to these classes, though, is the hands on experience; the sharing of experiences with others in the class; the ability to ask questions; and the boost in confidence from receiving a certificate.

If you find that these classes or programs are near you and the fee is reasonable for your budget, then you may be receiving guidance to attend. If the schedule doesn't work for you or is too cost prohibitive, then do not feel an obligation to go. As you learn to trust your gut, you will "feel" if it would benefit you to attend a certain course.

The point I'm making is that you can use your skill set to give readings even without a certification. I personally do not have a certification and was told that I don't need one right now. At some point, though, I may take classes so that I can learn more from the instructor or the other like minded individuals that will be in attendance. I know that there is always something we can learn from others!

As you work with your angels, they will guide you into what additional resources would benefit you. For now, just keep reading and you may have a better idea of what all is involved.

To have a clearer understanding in how a reading works, my angels want me to clarify some issues that are sometimes raised. Skeptics sometimes accuse psychics/intuitives of giving "cold readings". This type of reading is based solely on talking with and observing the client. The reader then relays information based on what is gleaned during that conversation and observation. There are readers who may do this and not be in communication with a supernatural source.

With that being said, my angels have told me that it is important to notice things about the client and use the information that you have learned about people in general during the reading. The angels will also guide you to notice something that is important during the reading. To sum it up, a reading combines knowledge that you have learned in this world with otherworldly information.

Keep in mind that the guidance will mostly be based on your personal knowledge. The more information that you have learned in general, the easier it is for the angels to deliver what you need to know. This is one of the many reasons that the angels want us to keep learning and this may involve pursuing a formal education. We then have a bigger database that they draw information from. They can deliver information that we are not familiar with but it will be sketchy to us and we won't understand it.

It is also good for us to learn about the world with its diversity of people and cultures as this helps us in tolerance and acceptance of others. Learning about economic systems enables us to have a better understanding of the world's resources and our role as participants within that system. Studying our ecosystem helps us to realize how all living and non-living things interact within our environment. With all of this knowledge, we can make good decisions towards creating a peaceful and healthy planet.

Since the world is ever changing, it is also important to keep up with current events. Our angels encourage us to listen to all sides of any issue and be open-minded. We may not be receiving all of the facts and can be swayed by propaganda if we are not careful. Propaganda does exist and is used to influence people into a particular way of thinking that does not accurately depict the truth. The biased information is distributed to serve the needs of the propagandist. If in doubt, ask your angels to guide you into more information or help you in "feeling" what is truthful.

There are several ways to give angel readings and you will eventually develop your own technique and style.

I consider mine just a general angel reading but may change this up in the future. Some readers develop specialty sessions. Examples would be "Past, Present and Future" readings, "Life Purpose" readings, "Soul Readings", "Mediumship Readings" etc. You may decide to find a specialty niche that you enjoy and work mainly in that area. As of right now, I am being advised that I may be doing "Archangel Michael Readings".

You may also decide to call yourself something other than an angel intuitive. The titles are important in that they relay information to your client about you. They may make a decision to book a reading based on your title so keep that in mind. The types of readings and how you identify yourself should be personalized for you but should always be based in love and light.

Also, please keep in mind that giving angel readings is a profession and you should dress accordingly. Do your best to avoid wearing too much black as most people associate this with negativity. When I first began giving readings, I had a lot of black and browns in my closet. My budget was tight and those colors are basic and matched most everything that I had. Plus, I always felt thinner when I wore them.

My angels advised me to add brighter colors as I was looking a bit gothic. They reminded me that persona is important and that I should send a message about myself even within my clothing. So . . . I went shopping! With that being said, money was a concern so I went to a few resale shops and watched for sales. My angels always steered me in the right direction to get exactly what I needed!

If at some point you decide to have business cards printed or a website designed, please choose wording and images that also radiate love and light. Incorporating anything that is generally accepted as "fearful," should be avoided. Examples of this would be using swords, blood, dragons, fire, etc. within your logo or other advertisement.

It is also important to pay attention to color schemes in your design. Using certain color combinations will send the wrong message. Although black can be used, it should be paired with rich colors that create an elegant feel. Red and black should always be avoided as they will be perceived as gothic and symbolic to blood and death. Your angels will guide you into colors that you will like and that will represent the message that they want you to send.

Now, here are some tips on how to actually do a reading:

1. Before you begin, place a few items of spiritual significance on a table or somewhere near you and your

client. Visuals are an important part of the reading and will help them feel at ease. Items can include crystals, angels, crosses, feathers or anything that helps create a sacred space. Also, be sure and have a pen and paper handy so that you can write down notes.

2. My angels have told me that it is also important to begin your session with a prayer of your choosing. The prayer is for your client's benefit as they may not be completely comfortable without it. Many people have a fear that a lower level energy could interfere in the reading or that you are not working completely in love and light. If you forget the prayer, do not worry. Rest assured that your pure intentions are enough. If it is important enough, your angels will somehow remind you to say it.

Here is a sample of a prayer to use before a session:

> *"Dear Heavenly Father, please bless those with us today. We ask for your love, guidance and protection. We ask that you send in your very best heavenly white light beings to deliver the information that this beautiful soul needs to know."*

> *"We also ask that if anyone on the other side wishes to communicate, that this*

> *communication be allowed to occur with your blessing. We ask that Archangel Azrael or Archangel Michael be the liaison for this communication. Thank you, dear Lord, Amen."*

3. After your prayer, write down the date and time and a few headings/topics that you feel are relevant to the type of reading that you are doing. Most people are interested in receiving information about subjects such as health, relationships and career so I usually use these headings. I also include a section that I call "Angel Talk" which encompasses teaching them about their spiritual connection.

   You don't really need these headings but may find it useful as a place to start. Some readers just start with the first word that "pops" into their head and begin talking based on that. I have also done readings like that as well.

   If you feel the need to do so, close your eyes to get a better connection. You may "see" an image that the angels would like you to start with or just have a general feeling about what needs to be covered.

4. Try to be aware of how long you have been talking during the reading and try not to run over what your

client has agreed upon. Just remember that your time is valuable and you may need your energy for another client. You can continue past the agreed upon time as long as your client has agreed to the additional fee (if you are charging) or you feel a strong need to cover additional information.

The angels are encouraging you to see this as a business and you should charge according to the standard rates in your area. As you gain experience, you will need to increase your fees. Giving readings is very time consuming and you should be paid accordingly. You may feel the need to give away information a time or two but rest assured that charging for your services is what the angels want you to do. This will allow you to be successful, expand your business and be able to help more people.

5. Be sure and allow a few extra minutes at the end of the reading to see if your client has questions. Alternatively, you can ask them at the beginning and write them down so that you cover them.

Although your readings will vary from person to person, there may be some similarities for many. The angels said not to be concerned about feeling like you are just repeating yourself. Many people will need some of the same information.

Encouragement to get more exercise, eat healthier, meditate and release worries are very common themes within many readings. For the most part, what will be different is how you direct them to accomplish these goals and the circumstances surrounding the issues that impede them. Just remember that you are going to be helping them heal physically, emotionally and spiritually.

As an example, if you feel like someone should be getting more exercise, you may "see" a bicycle in your mind's eye and encourage them to ride more; you may "feel" like dancing is important so you make a suggestion to them (or you may get a specific type of dancing "pop" into your mind); or you may "hear" the word "gym". As a side note, if you hear the word "gym", keep in mind that the spelling can also be "Jim", so always write down what else you think of as you talk. You can always go back and address it later or your client may immediately recognize the name. It may be someone in their present life that is living, can be a deceased person trying to connect through the angels, or it can be someone in their future.

You may also feel the need to discuss their diet and offer advice on changes that they can make. I would say that during most of my readings, my angels want me to address the processed and artificial foods that are in our society. I either advise them to avoid these, compliment them on their healthy food choices (if they are revealed to me) or encourage them to share the information with someone that they know. Sometimes the specifics come out during the reading and sometimes they do not. But, if I feel guided to discuss it, I do so. All of this type of information is helping you guide them into their physical healing.

You will also be able to help them heal their spiritual connection if this is a concern. There are many who have lost their faith and trust in a divine source and need to be reminded of what is available to them. Helping them to release their fears and develop their faith and trust can be very rewarding. You may also feel the need to teach them how to achieve their own personal connection through meditation.

The angels have told me that every one of us is "hard-wired" to have a divine connection but that it is up to us to develop it. We have to ask for help, make the necessary changes and trust that the divine world will deliver what we need. They are reminding me that we do have "free will", though, and can choose not to make those changes.

In many situations, you will be guided to address undesirable emotions that your client is holding on to.

You may experience the feelings briefly or simply think of a word that describes that feeling. Undesirable feelings such as worry, fear, anger, guilt, shame, blame, jealousy, etc. are impediments to our spiritual progression. You will be guided to help them with those feelings and relevant issues so that they can release them. Forgiveness of self and others will most likely be a part of this kind of reading. This is all a part of the emotional healing process that you will be allowed to assist them with.

You may not receive very detailed information such as names, dates or places so do not be concerned if this type of information does not come through. We are not here to necessarily impress people with unimportant details, but to share information that can change one's life for the better.

Be sure and trust your gut feeling as you deliver information and do not worry if it doesn't resonate with your client. Some information is prophetic or relevant to someone else that they will be talking to. The client may also discount your information as they may be in denial about certain things. Just remember, your angels are delivering what they need to know. Their epiphany about your accuracy may come later.

With experience and practice, you will not be concerned about this accuracy based on the "hits" that your client can confirm. It is very important to simply deliver what comes through. If you are in doubt, simply pause and ask your angels "Is this what you are wanting me to share?" and just go with your gut feeling about it.

Oftentimes the angels deliver information that is a bit of a puzzle. It can be cryptic and sometimes be frustrating for the reader and client. You do not need to interpret what you are delivering as it may be important for your client to figure it out later. The information frequently has overlapping meanings which can be quite impressive.

Many clients are also interested in connecting with someone who has passed away and will search out a medium. Although, most people associate mediums to be those that connect with the spirits of the deceased, the definition is a little different. A medium is one that is considered to be an intermediary between this world and the divine world. An angel intuitive is also a medium since they are the intermediary between humans and angels. They are also allowed to connect with the deceased with the angels serving as their liaison.

I personally believe that all angel intuitives can or will be able to connect with the deceased during their readings. If your client wants to talk with a spirit, then you can ask your angels to assist in the conversation. If that person does not come through, then you can reassure your client that it is not the appropriate time. We don't always know what is in our best interest but the angels certainly do.

If the person does come through, the information may be revealed in a variety of manners. You may smell something that was relevant to them, such as a certain perfume, cigar smoke, or a baked good. You may also "see" someone in your mind's eye. This can be best done with your eyes shut as the visual is easier to see. Many times, I can see a person like this and just feel or sense whether they are male or female and their relationship to the client. The angels may show me additional information if I need clarification of who it is.

As an example, I once saw an elderly man sitting in a recliner with a nasal cannula on, an oxygen tank on one side and a floor lamp on the other side. I began to describe this to the clients (there were two) and I felt like this was their father. The angels then drew my attention to the lamp, which puzzled me. I started to dismiss it and then they showed me the details of the lamp, including the pleated shade. I kept talking about it and realized that there was some significance to the lamp being turned off or on.

The clients became very excited when I relayed this information to them. This was exactly what they needed as confirmation that their deceased father was communicating with them. Apparently, one of the sisters recently had a very unusual experience with a light being turned on. She had believed that it was a sign from her dad and now she knew that it really was him!

Divination tools can also be used during a reading. There are several different types but the most common one that I know of is with cards. They can be either oracle or tarot cards, depending on your preference. Just be sure that the images on the cards that you use do not have any frightening images as this is not what the angels want. There are many different types of decks out there and you should choose the deck or decks that resonate with you. Angels, fairies, goddesses, the earth and Native American themes are just a few of them.

I believe that most of these decks have an instruction booklet included so it is a good idea to read it. Be sure and look over all the cards, noticing the many details about them. The cards serve as a trigger for your thought process in order to deliver a message that the angels want you to share. I don't use the cards, myself, but feel like a reader should always go with their gut instinct when using them, even if it contradicts information in the instruction booklet.

Many angel intuitives also gravitate towards other ways to heal besides readings. One of these ways is to perform energy work. Energy work or energy healing involves the transfer of supernatural energy through one person to another. This type of work allows the "life force" to assist your client with all levels of healing, although many seek it out for physical healing. As of now, much of this healing work cannot be proven scientifically, but I feel this will be changing in the future.

There are many forms of energy work with the most common ones being reiki, chakra healing and crystal therapy. You may feel a connection to one modality more than the others or you can learn them all. It is also not uncommon to make up your own healing method by combining what you like most about the other methods that you have learned.

The angels said not to be concerned about doing it exactly like you learned it. They may be guiding you into a different technique for the benefit of your clients. That technique can also change from client to client depending on what is in their best interest. I am no authority on any of the energy healing techniques but would like to share an overview of what I do know about them.

Reiki is a Japanese technique of delivering healing energy through the hands to another person. It is considered hands on healing and may involve touching the other person or the hands can be kept at a slight distance. The name is derived from two Japanese words, "Rei" which means "spiritual higher power" and "Ki" which means "life force energy". Thus, Reiki is considered to be "spiritually guided life force energy".

Chakra is a term associated with the ancient Indian language of Sanskrit and means wheel or disk. Chakras are considered to be energy points through which healing can occur. There are believed to be seven major chakras within the body that can become unbalanced and lead to illness. I'm oversimplifying this as I'm not very familiar with the chakras so you may want to do some further reading.

Crystal therapy is another method of energy healing and involves using various rocks, stones and crystals during a session. They can be used in conjunction with the chakra points or other points on the body. They may also be placed near someone during a session. Here again, I'm not very familiar with crystal therapy and would encourage you to do further reading on this.

During an energy healing session, your client may experience a variety of emotions. It is not uncommon for them to suddenly cry and release unhealthy emotions, such as guilt, grudges, prolonged grief, etc. They may have sudden awareness of the need to offer forgiveness to all, including themselves. They may also cry out of sheer joy when they feel the presence of divine beings and experience the feeling of unconditional love.

It is also not uncommon for the client to have visions within their mind's eye that also assist them in their healing. These visions can be of deceased loved ones that they need to find closure with or other beings from the other side who want to work with them.

The visions can also become out-of-body type experiences where the client is transported to another time and/or place. The purpose to these experiences is usually very complex and will always be for the benefit of the client. With that being said, don't discount the information that they share with you as it could also involve a special message for you!

My husband had a very interesting experience like this during an energy healing session while we were in Colorado. We had met the healer at a rock wholesale show and felt like we had been guided there. We both had sessions with her but his experience was far more impressive than mine.

She actually had three differently themed rooms set up with one of them having an Egyptian feel to it. According to my husband, shortly after she began to work on him, he felt like he was in Egypt. In his mind's eye, he could see the pyramids in great detail and felt like he was riding a camel. At some point, he could see himself in the reverse role as the healer performing energy work..

Although I'm not privy to understanding the entire meaning of this, I personally believe it helped him to understand better what his "mind's eye" is all about and to trust that the information that he received was external. I also think that it was a revelation of his future . . . to be a healer with his hands.

So now that you have a better understanding of what an angel intuitive does, you can decide whether this will be a hobby or a profession for you. Either way, you will be able to deliver healing information that will benefit everyone around you. Please remember, that with any skill set, practice is important. Just rest assured that your angels are with you every step of the way!

Also, be sure and be nice to your angels! They are here to serve us but are not our servants!

Chapter Nine

Myths and Superstitions

I wasn't originally going to include this as a chapter, but my angels advised me that it would be a good idea. People that work in the paranormal or metaphysical field are going to need to know how to deal with myths and superstitions. I will address a few general ones but the primary message here is the relationship between these myths and the concept of evil. I will present my own thoughts on the matter and leave you to decide what your own personal philosophy is. Regardless of whether you believe like I do, the angels want you to know that as a lightworker/healer that works within love and light, you are protected and have nothing to fear.

Have you ever been swayed by a superstition? If you are really honest, you will most likely say yes. I have found myself knocking on wood a time or two. Superstitions have been around a long time and are embedded in all different kinds of cultures. For the most part, the ideas concerning them are very similar.

The general consensus is that they involve a religious or spiritual belief system. This belief system was understood to be governed by mysterious rules and forces that could defy the laws of nature. What is interesting is that many of these superstitions have origins that contradict each other. For example, some cultures believe that the act of knocking on wood protects them from having something unfortunate happen. Other ones believe that it will simply bring good luck. So which is it? Well, I guess that depends on what your cultural background is and your overall attitude in general.

I would say that the majority though, tended to view superstitions with a fear of negativity. So, why are superstitions so heavily associated with negative repercussions? Let's take a better look at the history of one such superstition and the fear that is associated with it.

Since ancient times, people have believed in evil and punishment for their wrongdoings. For example, it was common for people in the Middle Ages to associate the plague as supernatural repercussions of their actions. Many also believed that the individual that was sick was possessed by demons. They did not have knowledge of disease and its effect on people. In other words, their level of understanding was very basic and somewhat primitive.

Although many at that time understood certain herbs to be medicinal, some did not. These folks believed that the herbs were only used to ward off evil spirits. In reality, these herbs were used to cleanse the bacteria out of the air and as respiratory treatments for the sick.

One such herb that has been scientifically studied is sage. It has been well documented to have numerous health benefits. Sage is known to have anti-bacterial, anti-viral, antioxidant and anti-inflammatory properties, just to name a few. Burning sage can dramatically clear up airborne bacteria and this benefit can last for many hours.

Sage is also being studied for its use in cognition and mood disorders; diabetes; and as a treatment for menopause. Even though it has wonderful medicinal benefits, many still believe its most valuable asset, though, is in clearing out negativity and evil.

My angels have told me that the burning of sage to get rid of evil spirits or negativity is considered a superstition and not necessary. With that in mind, though, you may have clients that want you to burn sage to cleanse their home. If this happens, you can burn the sage so that they feel more protected. It might also be a great time to share the medicinal benefits with them!

It is also a good idea to offer a blessing as you go through their home. Just remember, that your angelic connection is what gives people peace of mind!

As far as evil is concerned, my personal belief is that it is generated by humans and not an otherworldly source. It develops when people lose their way and turn away from our Creator who wants us to be loving beings. These lost souls on earth have lost their connection with Source and can no longer receive the direction and guidance that He is providing. They become egocentric, greedy and power hungry and their actions lead to discord and chaos. It is this kind of evil that we are battling on earth.

As a healer, your loving guidance can help those that are misguided, either one at a time or one thousand. Your prayers and loving intentions can also send positive vibrations that cannot be seen but can absolutely make a difference.

I also believe that perspective is important when thinking about evil and negative energies. I believe that there will be times when we perceive something as evil but it is really not. To get a better understanding of this viewpoint, I'd like to share my experience with a house cleansing and a supposed evil entity. You can then decide for yourself what happened.

Sometime last year, I received a phone call to assist in getting rid of an evil entity. One of the residents claimed that she was choked during her nap and thus a call for help was made by her mother to rid the place of this evil spirit. She had called a prominent ghost tour guide in our area, who, in turn called me to see if I wanted to help. I discussed this briefly with my angels and agreed to go. I never felt a sense of dread or any negativity and wondered what was going on. My angels told me not to worry about anything and that I would understand when I got there.

As soon as I entered their home, I realized what they meant. The curtains were all closed so it was very dark inside. I noticed that there were numerous video games near the television and they were all of a violent nature. As I passed a bookcase, my angels drew my attention to the titles and most of them were horror based or just plain morbid. They also drew my attention to the victim's boyfriend and I noticed that he was wearing a black T-shirt with a skull on it and he was overweight. He also looked very sad.

There were two bedrooms in this tiny home and they showed me the one where the choking had occurred. I walked in and felt nothing strange. My gut feeling was that this woman was a smoker and that she had an asthma attack. She admitted that she smoked and that she did indeed have asthma, but denied that she had an attack from it. She steadfastly claimed that she felt someone choking her.

I then passed the other bedroom door that was closed and sensed something very wrong. I asked if we could go in so she knocked on the door. The room belonged to her boyfriend's teenage son who was inside playing a hand held video game. He barely looked up and didn't acknowledge our presence, even when spoken to. My gut told me that this was the problem.

I learned that the boy had brought home a deck of tarot cards that afternoon and they asked if this could be the source of the attack. I assured them that it was not, but I feel that this card deck may have served some purpose. I feel like there is sometimes some very creative divine orchestration to help people get what they need.

I also felt like there was a major problem between the father and son and this was confirmed. I discussed this with the dad and made several suggestions on how to address it. I also made suggestions to the dad on how to deal with his depression, which he admitted was another problem.

I knew that I needed to speak with the son but wasn't sure what I was going to say. All I know is that my angels had not let me down and the right words would come to me. I briefly explained about my miraculous physical healing and my clairaudient gift of hearing angel voices.

Up until this point, he had been playing his video game and completely inattentive of our conversation. But when I began talking about the angel voices in musical terms, he stopped what he was doing and looked at me. I finished up my story, knowing that I needed to keep it brief.

After I left, I wondered what had happened. I know that I must have had some kind of positive impact on all of them that day or I would not have been sent there. Remember the suicide story from a previous chapter? I do know that we can be guided to be at the right place at the right time.

In all reality, I will probably never know what all happened after that. Did the family get the help they needed? How big of a crisis was this? And, in all reality, it simply doesn't matter whether I know or not. What I do know is that I learned a valuable lesson that day so that I can pass it along to others.

I believe the lesson I learned is that there will be times that God has to use extraordinary measures to deliver the healing that people need. It also has to be delivered in terms that they understand and will take action on. In this situation, a family in crisis believed in evil and this is what prompted them to reach out for help.

Although this is my understanding of the events, there can be another interpretation of what happened. There may have been an actual evil entity present within that home. This entity could have been drawn in by the negative atmosphere of the home and was up to no good. God may have decided to send one of his lightworkers in to get rid of the evil entity.

The only problem that I see with the second interpretation is that the idea of evil beings creates fear. This is in direct contradiction to all of the messages that I have ever received. Living in fear causes distress which causes unhappiness and this is not what God wants for us. We are supposed to be happy and live without fear.

I believe that as a part of our spiritual progression, we are being guided to release these fears as they no longer serve a purpose. Remember the definition of enlightenment? "Enlightened beings live their lives in a blessed state and are optimistic and full of positivity; live without fear and worry; and trust in a Universal Energy Source to take care of their earthly needs."

Fear can also spread to others around us. This is what is known as the ripple effect. Let me explain . .

Have you ever thrown a rock into a calm lake just to watch the ripples on the water? As you study it, you can see the concentric rings that form around the point of entrance. These rings expand exponentially and spread out over other areas of the lake in direct proportion to the size of the rock that was tossed in.

If you throw in many small pebbles you will see these rings bump into each other, one influencing the next, based on their individual sizes. These effects are known as ripple effects. It is where one action or event influences the area around it, causing a series of other events to happen.

If you study sociology, you will find that people can also be participants in the ripple effect. Our words and actions can heavily influence those around us, creating a chain of events and repercussions that we may or may not be aware of.

Think about what type of ripple effect that you want to have on others. Do you want to spread positivity or spread negativity? Do you want to comfort those around you or incite them into being more fearful? Do you want to spread calmness or add to the chaos?

People should choose their words and actions very carefully. They can be the drop that creates a wave of positive change or the one that adds to a turbulent sea.

Ultimately, it is up to you as to what you believe about negativity and evil entities. I am simply sharing other ideas and perspectives that my angels have taught me. Perhaps it is time to discard old beliefs that no longer serve your highest good. Just remember, your role as a lightworker is to make a positive difference on this planet so always spread messages of love and light!

Chapter Ten

Who are the Archangels?

As I write this book, I am approaching the fifth anniversary of my miraculous healing. During the last five years I have spent many hours in meditation, giving gratitude and also additional requests. One of those requests has been to get to know each of the archangels on an individual basis.

My goal is to be able to recognize them based on their individual characteristics and to teach others to do the same. There are many ways to identify them, some of which are by colors, personalities and what their teaching specialties are. As of now, this request has not been entirely granted as I only know a few of them quite well.

The one archangel that I am particularly close to is Archangel Ariel. She has identified herself as my guardian angel although I didn't believe her at first. In all reality, I didn't feel that I was worthy to have an archangel in this role. I have since learned otherwise. I am sharing this with you as I believe that many of you lightworkers will have Archangels as your own guardian angels. I am being told that your mission in this lifetime is very important so please don't discount the information.

The bulk of this chapter will be based on what I have learned about each of the archangels from various sources and from what I would call hearsay. This hearsay will be secondhand information coming from the angels that work closely with me. For now, this is good enough for me.

UPDATE! While doing more research on the archangels for this chapter, I have felt an enormous amount of additional information coming through from each one! I believe that my lesson here is about timing, patience and research. The angels want us to gather as much information about them as we can and they will provide the rest!

Before we learn about each archangel, I'd like to share additional information that I stumbled on to. It involves four angels in particular who are known as the Four Cardinal Angels. Some believe that these angels represent the elements of earth, fire, air and water. These angels are also believed to oversee the earth's four cardinal points of North, South, East and West.

The word cardinal originates from the Latin language and means chief or key. With this definition, we assume that anything cardinal is also significant and essential. Therefore, the definition of a cardinal angel is the "chief or highest in the hierarchy of archangels". The following is a list of these angels and their duties.

Michael – associated with the direction of South and with the element of fire. Michael is believed to be the head of the four cardinal angels and teaches us about truth and courage.

Gabriel – associated with the direction of West and the element of water. Gabriel is the communicator that assists us in understanding God's messages.

Raphael – associated with the direction of East and the element of air. Raphael assists us in healing our mind, body and soul.

Uriel – associated with the direction of North and the element of earth. Uriel is the archangel that helps us gain knowledge and wisdom.

Keep in mind as you study the rest of this chapter that these four angels may present to you with the learned associations above. They can use their associated direction and element or simply the red bird, cardinal, to let you know that they are present with you. It may be useful to use this information in combination with the rest of this chapter in identifying who is working with you. Now, let's take a look at all of the archangels in greater detail.

Ariel

The name Ariel means "Lioness of God" and this angel will present as a strong powerful female energy. She represents the qualities of courage, strength and confidence. She is also believed to be the angel that can assist us with prosperity.

Ariel is also associated with the earth elements of air (including wind) and water. She is closely connected with all things in nature, particularly birds. Since she is closely connected with nature, she is a strong advocate for preserving the environment.

She works closely with Archangel Raphael and encourages us to go outside more, relax and enjoy the magical healing atmosphere of the natural world around us. Ariel is also associated with the nature elementals which are considered to be fairies, nature spirits, sprites, etc.

Although I have studied her associated color to be a pale pink energy, I personally have not experienced this. When I think of Ariel, I see the color green with a secondary color of yellow. Perhaps it is because she is so strongly associated with nature (green grass); money (also green) and the environment (think about going green). Her association with Archangel Raphael (whose color is green) also lends credence as to why I perceive her this way. To me, the yellow represents the sun (outdoors) and is also to clarify that it is her and not Raphael

At any rate, my angels told me that each individual may identify a different color or set of colors for the archangels depending on their own thought process and associated learnings. For me to completely memorize something, I like to have an association of some kind.

With that in mind, I also "see" her as having red hair and I attribute this to a fictional movie with a particularly adventuresome mermaid character.

I believe that the Archangels may also present with animals including those linked with Native American Indians. Since Ariel means "Lioness of God", I feel like the lioness would naturally be her animal. She will also likely present with small animals and birds of all kinds around her since she is connected to the outdoors.

Her associated stone is believed to be rose quartz but here again, my thoughts differ. I believe that a yellow stone such as citrine would be connected to her although this is an overlap with Archangel Gabriel's stone. Either way, the angels always remind me that it is about intention and what your instinct tells you.

Azrael

The name Azrael means "God's Help" or "Whom God Helps" and this angel will present as a male energy. He is sometimes referred to as the "Angel of Death" although I would refer to him as the "Transition Angel".

He assists those that are departing this earthly plane and comforts those that are left behind. With this in mind, he is strongly associated with grief counselors and can assist those desiring to work in mediumship.

He helps those having issues of forgiveness, guilt, anger and regret that are connected to a departed loved one. These are strong and undesirable emotions that do not serve our higher good and Azrael is here to help.

He also assists the new arrivals which are those souls that are transitioning into this world. He may present in this manner along with Archangel Gabriel to welcome a new baby.

Another role of Azrael concerns grief and transitions in general. Any kind of loss can create grief that needs to be dealt with. His presence can provide comfort and guidance during these types of transitions and he may be accompanied by another archangel that can further assist you.

His associated color is believed to be creamy white or pale yellow but my perception is slightly different. I had a profound experience when my mother-in-law passed away where I saw a rainbow as she crossed into heaven. With that in mind, my association with Azrael is primarily a rainbow (also associated with Raziel) and the color black presenting secondarily.

Although many consider the color black indicative of doom and gloom or evil, I can assure you that it is most definitely not. In our society, black is worn at funerals and during times of mourning as a cultural sign of respect so its natural association would be with death. Should you "see" black and feel Azrael's presence, please have no fear. He is trying to teach us to not think so negatively and also not to give in to old superstitions regarding evil. Black is an easy color to perceive and is a quick way for him to identify himself. It would also not be confused with any of the other archangel's colors.

He has also shown me a picture of the grim reaper which did not bother me at all. He will usually add a touch of humor somewhere within his presentation. Here again, he will present to you based on your personal comfort level and your own experiences.

I believe that Azrael's associated animal would be the white dove which represents peace. Although the normal association is "peace on earth", the dove can represent a peaceful transition from this world to heaven. Another animal that Azrael may show you is the zebra. Its black and white stripes appear to be never ending on the zebra's body and could signify eternal life and death. One additional animal that may present with Azrael is the stork because of its association with new babies. Just remember that Azrael welcomes new souls as they enter this earth!

His stone association is said to be with yellow calcite but I tend to think about rainbow obsidian in relation to him. This stone is black with a slight rainbow of other colors within it. This was the stone that he showed me that I could associate with him. He also showed me Dalmatian jasper which is white with black spots on it just like the dog!

Chamuel

The name Chamuel means "He Who Sees God" and this angel may present as a male energy. At this time, though, I don't perceive this angel as being male or female. It is possible that I have not worked with this angel very much or he/she does not want to present with a gender.

Chamuel's mission is to help individuals find inner peace which ultimately creates universal peace. With that in mind, his focus is on love and teaching us to release our fear based thinking. It is this lower level energy (that we produce) that impedes our spiritual progress.

In addition to helping us find inner peace, he can assist us in finding whatever else we are looking for. This includes finding out what our life purpose is; finding a better job, relationship or home; and assisting us in finding lost items.

With Chamuel's help, we can raise the vibration of our planet through creating healthy relationships of all kinds. Since this angel is so strongly connected with love, I have to wonder if he is the equivalent to what we know as Cupid. This may be one way that he presents to you unless you identify this with another archangel.

Archangel Chamuel wants to remind us to live our lives in a loving state. This means that all of our thoughts and actions should be based on love. If you are saying or doing things without loving intentions, then Chamuel is encouraging you to make changes. It is this basic love that can heal the world.

Archangel Chamuel may present to you with an animal that will have an association to what he is trying to teach us. Since he is strongly linked to peace, I believe that his animal is also the white dove. To avoid confusion with Archangel Azrael, ask for clarification and pay attention to other information that you perceive at the same time.

The color that is associated with Chamuel is pale green and the gemstone association is with fluorite. Because of his association with love, I feel a light pink loving energy when he is around and think about hearts. If you have a different experience, just trust your gut instinct and ask for clarification as to whom you are working with. The angels love us to learn and solve the little mysteries!

Gabriel

The name Gabriel means "Strength of God" and this angel may present as male or female. The most recent artistic depictions of Gabriel are of a female being with a long flowing gown and a trumpet. She is believed to be one of the Four Cardinal Angels, although her personal association in that context may be male.

Gabriel is known as the supreme messenger of God and has delivered prophetic messages to the people regarding the birth of Jesus as well as John the Baptist. Because of this, she is closely connected to Jesus and Mother Mary.

With her role as communicator, she assists those in areas of communication, creative expression and the arts. She can also assist you if your desire is to work with children in some capacity.

The animal that I believe could be associated with Archangel Gabriel is the sheep because of its association to her announcement of the birth of Jesus. It could also be the elephant because of the "trumpeting" sounds they make. She may also present with any yellow colored animal such as a Golden Retriever, etc. since her color association is yellow or gold. One more alternative that she is showing me is that of the crowing rooster because of its distinct association with the announcement of morning.

Gabriel will most likely present with a copper or gold color, much like that associated with the trumpet. Her stone association is believed to be citrine and she is also connected to the metals gold and copper.

Haniel

The name Haniel means "Grace of God" and this angel presents with a clear feminine energy. She is considered the angel closely connected to the moon and stars with ties to astronomy and astrology.

She also has a strong association with assisting women in finding their own divine self and helping with other female issues.

Haniel is also available to help those that are interested in developing their intuitive gifts, specifically clairvoyance. This is a slight overlap with Archangels Raziel and Jeremiel who also help us develop this gift. You can ask in general for help and one of these angels is sure to show up!

The animal that I believe would be closely associated with Haniel would be the wolf due to its close ties to the moon within Native American culture. The owl could be another animal that will present with her since it is a nocturnal animal.

She presents with the pale blue color of moonlight and is linked to the gemstone moonstone. Another gemstone that may be linked to her is blue lace agate due to its pale blue color. She is telling me that since the moonlight can be of a pale yellow color, look for this as well. She knows it is an overlap with Archangel Uriel, but you will feel her distinct female presence and most likely "see" a moon or the nighttime sky within your mind's eye to further identify her.

She is asking me to share an interesting little tidbit with you. While working on this chapter, I realized that we experienced a rare lunar event. On Monday, June 20, 2016, we experienced a full moon that coincided with the summer solstice. (The summer solstice is the first day of summer and the longest day of the year). The timing of these two events created what is known as a solstice full moon and this hasn't happened since 1948!

As I researched a bit more I discovered that the June full moon is also known as the Strawberry Moon since June is believed to be the best time to harvest strawberries. So this means that we had a Strawberry Solstice Full Moon!

If you are fond of astronomy, just ask Haniel to guide you into other interesting information and she will most graciously oblige. I am also being informed that she can take you on an interesting celestial trip if you so desire!

Jeremiel

The name Jeremiel means "Mercy of God" and this angel presents as a male energy. This angel's specialty is assisting us with what's known as a "living life review" so you can make changes on how you want to live your life. Much of this deals with understanding our past, working through forgiveness issues and releasing unwanted negative emotions so we can be free of these burdens. Archangel Raziel can also help us with this review and typically helps us to see the humor in it.

Because of his role in working with us through this life review, Jeremiel is closely linked to the gift of clairvoyance, which means "clear seeing". He can help with your review by showing you visual images that are relevant to your personal lessons. Many times this is done gradually without you realizing that you are being schooled. If you are recalling memories that bring up undesired emotions, then Jeremiel is assisting you with finding resolution.

Jeremiel also assists the recently departed souls go through their life review before they ascend to Heaven. Because of this, he works closely with Archangel Azrael.

The animal most likely to present with Jeremiel is the butterfly because of its capability of transformation.

He is showing me that as we go through our living life review and heal, we are transforming into a happy healthy state of being. With his help, our tightly wrapped cocoon can open up, releasing painful emotions and allowing our beautiful free spirit to emerge.

He is also showing me a pair of eyes on the upper wings of a beautiful multi-colored butterfly. This is representative of his job to assist us with our clairvoyant gift of "clear seeing".

Jeremiel is believed to present with a dark purple color that can easily be confused with the blue violet color associated with Michael or the navy blue color associated with Zadkiel. It is best to ask for clarification from Archangel Jeremiel and he will send you the additional information that you need to identify his presence.

The stone that is associated with him is amethyst but may be different for you. There are many purple stones out there so you may need to just set your intention on which one connects you to Jeremiel.

Jophiel

The name Jophiel means "Beauty of God" and she has a distinct female energy. Her job is to bring beauty into our world, whether it is personal or work related.

She helps us with organization and tidiness so that our surroundings can be pleasant. She also helps us with keeping our thoughts positive and filling our heart with gratitude.

Jophiel is associated with the color dark pink, fuchsia or rose pink which can easily be confused with Archangel Metatron (dark pink & green) or Archangel Ariel (if she presents to you with rose pink). Ask for clarification and pay attention to other thoughts or feelings that pop into your head to distinguish who is connecting with you.

Jophiel may also present with an animal so that you can further identify her or to learn a lesson that she would like to share. She may present with solid colored pink birds such as flamingos or any other brightly colored birds (such as peacocks) that are considered beautiful. She may also present with brightly colored fish as well.

Also, if you are drawn to look at something beautiful, she is probably guiding you into it simply for your enjoyment!

Since Jophiel has a strong tie to pink, common stone associations are of the same color. Pink tourmaline or any pink stone can be a means of connecting with Jophiel.

Metatron

Metatron is one of two archangels that are believed to have walked on earth in human form. He presents with a strong male energy and is believed to have been the scribe, Enoch from biblical times. Enoch was believed to be a very honest scholar in divine wisdom. It is also said that Metatron sits on the right side of God, although I usually see Jesus at the right side of God. I am being told by Metatron that he is simply waiting in the wings behind Jesus. Hmmm, I believe that was more angel humor.

Metatron is commonly associated with sacred geometry and the Merkabah cube for healing. His role is to impart divine knowledge and he is believed to work with sensitive children as well as adults. Sensitive children are those considered to be Indigo, Crystal and Rainbow children. Many of these are adults now and Metatron continues to work with them.

Since Metatron was once a scribe, he is also believed to be the keeper of the Book of Life (Akashic Records). In this capacity, he assists those involved in any kind of record keeping as well as writers.

The colors that are associated with Metatron are green and deep pink/violet and can be metallic looking. I was taught that watermelon tourmaline is associated with him but feel there are other stones that will work as well. A stone known as peacock ore which is multicolored and metallic can also be connected with him. Any other metallic rock can be used as well to feel a connection to Metatron.

Because of his connection to geometry, the animal most likely to present with Metatron is the spider within a web. Yes, I can't believe that I am being shown a spider. I personally do not like them and have asked him to present without this visual image. He has told me that I need to get over my fear and he will change the image when I do so.

He is reminding me that spiders are still God's living creations and that they have purpose in our world. Should I need to empower myself, he suggests that I visualize myself stepping on it. As of right now, I'm still finding some difficulty with this lesson but I must say that I'm amused. The one time that I stepped on a spider, I released thousands of baby spiders. Well, you can probably guess how that went.

Another animal that may present with Metatron is the peacock. The connection here is mostly because of the connection to the "peacock ore" stone mentioned above. I happen to have a very large peacock ore stone that is very metallic looking and I think of Metatron whenever I look at it. Just remember, though, that your experiences may differ based on what you have exposure or access to.

<u>Michael</u>

The name Michael means "He Who Is Like God" and he is the most well known of all the archangels. He is also considered the leader of the Four Cardinal Angels. He is depicted as a young athletic angel with a sword and shield. Both of these accessories are associated with battle, with the sword's purpose of slaying the ego and fear. With these weapons, he assists people in conquering their own fears and helping them to feel protected. As a protector, Michael helps us find our courage and inner strength to face life challenges.

I am being told that Archangel Michael may be changing his persona a bit by not presenting with the sword. The sword is a weapon and serves as a reminder of fear and battle. I believe that if you connect with him, he will present with his shield (particularly a round one) only and maybe a breastplate.

In my personal connection, I do not normally see Michael with a sword. I see him as a young strong male holding a round shield. The shield is the only representation that is necessary to know that it is him.

He works with anyone that calls upon him but has a close connection to "empaths" and those working on their clairsentient skills. He encourages us to shield ourselves from our own negative thoughts and those from the outside world. We are encouraged to stay positive about everything and it is in this manner that we are protected. The round shield can also represent the "bubble" that many envision as protection for themselves from negativity.

I am also being told that there is a connection with the round shield and a dreamcatcher from Native American folklore. Keep in mind that the interpretation of what a dreamcatcher is can vary and he is advising us to keep our thoughts positive in relation to it. He may present with a dreamcatcher type shield as well as a power animal. I believe that the animal associated with Archangel Michael is most likely the lion but he may present to you with a wolf, a stallion or a falcon.

Michael has a well known association with blue and purple and may present with either color or a combination of both. He can also present with a golden light that is representative as a flash of his sword. He is now showing me that he may present with the sword in the beginning and you may see him lay it on the ground. He will direct your focus to his shield so that this new image will allow you to know that it is him.

I personally envision Michael with having a distinct bluish purple color so that I don't get him confused with Archangel Zadkiel who presents with a darker navy blue color. As you work with the archangels, just take a few notes as to what you are seeing, thinking and feeling. It will be within these notes that you learn who is working with you.

Michael is well known to assist those working in dangerous occupations such as law enforcement, fire fighting and the military. Many men feel a strong connection to Archangel Michael because he represents strength and power. As these men progress past these earthly concerns, they generally will feel a connection to the female persona archangels as well.

I have learned that Michael is associated with the stone, sugilite which is primarily a purple stone. Personally, I do not envision him as being connected to this stone since it is just purple. I see him as having a connection to sapphires and tanzanite because of their blue-purple colors. He would like me to let you know that it is not necessary to purchase these stones to connect with him as they are expensive. If you would like a stone to use in this manner, simply pick out an inexpensive one of any color that you are drawn to.

Selenite is another stone that is believed to be connected to him and represents protection. Selenite is available in many forms, including lamps, sticks, towers and small polished stones and most are very affordable.

Raguel

The name Raguel means "Friend of God" and he presents as a male energy. He is the angel that assists us with harmony, peace, justice and fairness concerning our relationships with others as well as ourselves. In this capacity, he works with therapists and counselors in healing relationship issues. He also can work with those in the dispensing of justice such as lawyers, judges and others in the legal field.

The animal that I am being shown that best represents Raguel is the dolphin as it represents harmony, friendship and balance. This also makes sense to me as the associated color with Raguel is a deep pale blue color and the crystal aquamarine. The word aquamarine comes from "aqua marinus" which is Latin for "water of the sea".

Because this light blue color can be confused with Archangel Haniel, just ask Raguel to show you other identifiers so that you can recognize him. He may also present in your mind's eye by holding the "scales of justice" or you may just simply see the scales without an image of him.

Raguel is believed to be the angel to call on to enhance your clairsentient skills. As a reminder, the clairsentient skill is associated with your sense of touch or emotional feeling. Personally, I believe that Archangel Michael would be a better fit for this as he is the one that teaches us how to recognize and protect ourselves from our own negative thoughts and feelings. Archangels Michael and Raguel would like me to let you know, though, that any of the archangels can assist you with this gift.

Raphael

The name Raphael means "He Who Heals Like God" and presents as a male energy. He is well known as the supreme healing angel as well as one of the Four Cardinal Angels. He works to assist those in healing physical, spiritual and emotional issues.

Raphael works closely with anyone involved in the traditional healing field, including doctors, nurses, dentists, therapists, etc. He also works with those in alternative health fields such as acupuncturists, chiropractors, energy healers, etc.

Raphael is also believed to help with all aspects of physical travel by guiding those who request his assistance. He can also assist those that request his help in their spiritual journey here on earth.

The color emerald green is strongly associated with Raphael and his stones are believed to be emerald and malachite. Because these stones are expensive, I believe that any green stone, such as green quartz or aventurine can be connected to him.

An animal that may be associated with Raphael is the snake since it is found on the caduceus. The caduceus has long been a symbol of medicine and includes a winged staff with two snakes wrapped around it. Raphael may present to you with this symbol even if you are afraid of snakes. His goal would be to help you heal your fear of them.

I have envisioned and dreamed of snakes many times until I understood what was happening. I realized that there was an Archangel present and that nothing would happen to me. Raphael also showed me in my mind's eye on how to take charge of the situation.

I also see Raphael with a small white bird and a medicine pouch, much like the Native American Indians used to carry. He may carry it across his shoulder with a wide sash that is easily recognizable or a thinner leather one. When he is around, you may feel the presence of a strong medicine man. He is also telling me that you may smell some of the medicinal herbs that are common in your area.

Raphael is also showing me that he may present to you with a stethoscope or the large round medical head lamp/reflector that was worn many years ago. He said that these items are easily identifiable and are also connected to the healing field.

When I feel Raphael's presence, I sense the color green and do not always see it in my mind's eye. By sensing it, I just think about an emerald green color without any secondary colors. This is just one of the many ways that our angels will present to us!

Because Raphael is one of the Four Cardinal Angels, he could also present with a red cardinal. This would almost give a Christmas feel to his arrival because of his strong presence with the color green. This could be confusing with the presence of Archangel Gabriel who has strong ties to this holiday so look for other signs to determine who is present. I must say that the angels will really challenge us when it comes to learning who they are. Don't be surprised if you feel a little bit like you are taking a test when they begin to present to you.

I'd like to add here that I believe it was Raphael who guided me into drinking green tea every day and to share this with others. We have a lot of toxins in our environment and green tea is an inexpensive and easy way to get daily protection. He also suggests that if caffeine bothers you, to simply use the decaffeinated variety. He also would like you to try different brands if you do not like the taste or blend it with another flavored tea.

Raziel

The name Raziel means "Secrets of God" and his persona is of a wise old male wizard. He teaches us wisdom either by directing us to find knowledge or in helping us with resolution to painful memories. Just like Jeremiel, Raziel can show us our "living life review" if we request his help. This review helps us to see the past in a different light, whereby we can forgive ourselves and others. We can also gain compassion and enhance our empathy skills by this review.

Raziel can also assist us in uncovering memories from another lifetime and can be called upon during past life regression therapy. This knowledge can be used to improve the quality of our current lives.

As a wizard-like angel, Raziel can manifest to you in various forms. He can appear as a wise old man or a fun loving magical angel. My personal experience with him is in the latter persona and he has identified himself to me as "Razzy". I believe that he was one of the first angels that presented to me before I became clairaudient but I didn't know who he was.

During a meditation to connect with the angels, I distinctly remember seeing a very tiny, joyful angel with a small wand in my mind's eye. This angel playfully presented on my left side, dressed in a long white gown behaving more like Tinkerbell than an angel. He was doing somersaults and waving his wand. I also remember thinking about a television commercial from many years back where an actress, dressed in all white, portrayed herself as Mother Nature. I'm still not quite sure why this image and thought popped into my head.

Like the other archangels, Raziel can also present to you with an animal. This animal can be an owl due to their association with wisdom (wise old owl). He can also present with a more fun loving animal such as a magical unicorn.

Raziel is associated with the rainbow colors and his stone is believed to be clear quartz. He is presently showing me that a clear quartz stone with a rainbow will help one feel connected to him. Raziel, like Archangel Jeremiel, is believed to assist those with their clairvoyant skills (clear seeing) so call on him if you need help.

Sandalphon

Sandalphon is the second archangel that is believed to have once walked on earth in human form. He is considered to be the twin brother of Metatron and was known on earth as the prophet, Elijah. He presents as a male energy.

Several religious documents refer to Sandalphon as the deliverer of prayers from earth to heaven so he is known as an intercessor between humans and God. He is also known as the tallest of angels with his height extending from earth to heaven.

Sandalphon is also believed to lend his assistance to those in the musical field, including singers, composers and musicians. With his strong association to music, Sandalphon can assist those in healing through sound therapy.

One animal that I believe could be associated with Sandalphon would be the giraffe due to its height. Another animal could be the hawk due to its association with clear vision. Because of his lofty vantage point, it is believed that Sandalphon is able to see everything quite clearly.

The color and stone turquoise are commonly linked to Archangel Sandalphon, although your perception may be very different. Because of the varying nature of turquoise, pay attention to other signs that are associated with this angel when determining who is present.

When I "see" Sandalphon in my mind's eye, I see a very tall thin angel within a beach scene. I can sense a light turquoise and tan color around me. I also think immediately of Jesus, walking along the beach, leaving his footprints in the sand.

He is telling me that he presents to me like this because I can remember learned associations better. The words "sand" and "sandal" are within his name which references the beach and Jesus to me. I think he is showing me Jesus so that I can remember that he (Sandalphon) once walked on earth as well. He is not giving me the rest of the information as to why this is important so I guess I'll be patient and await that lesson later!

Another interesting piece of information that he is drawing my attention to is the last four letters of his name. Since "phon" is a musical term, I can now easily remember that he helps musicians of all kinds!

I can also recall the color that is associated with Sandalphon through these associations. All he has to do is show me the water at the beach and I can see it as turquoise blue! This is slightly confusing with Archangel Raguel so be sure and look for the other identifiers to determine who is connecting!

Uriel

The name Uriel means "He Who Is The Light of God" and he is considered one of the Four Cardinal Angels. He presents as a male energy; is associated with illumination; and is linked to divine insight and knowledge. He helps us with those "light bulb" moments which can also be called epiphanies.

Uriel is strongly associated with intellect and encourages us to educate ourselves. He reminds us that knowledge is power and can help us on our spiritual journey on earth. He can assist those that are pursuing an education or simply desire an answer to a problem.

He is the angel to call in if you want to further develop your claircognizant gift. This is the intuitive gift of "clear knowing" and he is more than happy to assist.

Paintings and drawings typically depict Uriel as holding a light, much like the Statue of Liberty here in the United States. This light is very symbolic of leadership, illumination, strength, clarity and focus. It can also be symbolic as the lighted pathway to God.

Uriel could be associated with the wolf as this animal symbolizes intelligence. Another animal that could be associated with him is the owl because of its association with learned knowledge. A third animal (and the one I like the best) that can signal Uriel's presence is the firefly due to its ability to glow with a light yellow light!

The associated color with Uriel is light yellow, much like the pale yellow light of a lit candle. His associated stone is amber which can be pale yellow, orange or light green. Any stone that has a yellow cast or is off white can be associated with Uriel.

Zadkiel

Zadkiel's name means "Righteousness of God" and he is known as the benevolence angel. He presents as a male energy and is also associated with compassion, forgiveness, freedom and mercy.

Zadkiel also helps us with memory and can help students in school or anyone with memory problems. It is in this capacity that he helps people heal from painful memories. He will show you how to offer forgiveness to everyone. This allows people to realize and enjoy their life purpose and no longer be a victim of their own negative thoughts.

A deep indigo blue that is close to navy is the color that is associated with Zadkiel. This color can be confused with that of Archangel Michael so ask for clarification if you are seeing a lot of dark blue around you. Any dark blue stone can help with your connection to him, although lapis lazuli is considered his stone.

The animal that I associate with Zadkiel is the eagle because it is a symbol of freedom in the United States. Because he also works with those with memory issues, he may present with an elephant. These animals are well known to have a very good memory.

Zadkiel is also the archangel who can assist you in developing your clairaudient gift. He encourages us to sit quietly and listen to white noise, thus conditioning our auditory nerve. He is reminding me that white noise can be made by fans, air conditioners, washers, dryers, dishwashers or any device that has a hum. Pay attention to any sounds that are not a part of the white noise that you are hearing.

He also recommends that you go outdoors and listen to the sounds of nature. Some of those sounds may just be your angels communicating with you. They can even sound a lot like happy little birds chirping away! Sometimes the angels will even speak to you through the wind as it blows through the trees or within the melody of outdoor windchimes. These are all just a few of my personal experiences!

Nathaniel

Archangel Nathaniel is considered a newcomer to the archangel group but that is only because he has not revealed himself to many people just yet. His name means "Gift of God" and it is believed that he revealed himself around the year 2012 to assist lightworkers with the spiritual shifts that would begin around this time.

Nathaniel is considered to be a strong forceful angel that encourages us to take action in fulfilling our heart's desire. He helps us release self-doubt and find confidence in our spiritual gifts. He also encourages us to get out of our comfort zone and may push us into this a time or two for our own good.

Although it is good to continue our metaphysical studies, Nathaniel also encourages us to begin practicing our healing on others and stop procrastinating. This will give us experience and is the best way to really understand how it works. I believe that it was Archangel Nathaniel who strongly encouraged me to begin doing readings back in 2012, even though I didn't feel prepared. I know now that it is through practice that we get better and build our confidence.

The animal that I would most associate with Nathaniel would be the tiger. The tiger is a symbol of personal strength and can serve as a catalyst for energy and change. It was used as a marketing tool many years ago whereby "putting a tiger in your tank" meant to fill your tank with energy. Tigers are also associated with assertiveness and this is what Nathaniel is trying to teach us.

Nathaniel could also be associated with the Phoenix which is a mythical bird. It has an association with fire and is a symbol of strength and rebirth. As lightworkers wake up to their spiritual gifts, Nathaniel is there to assist them in discovering who they truly are and getting comfortable with this new self.

Nathaniel is associated with the color red; the sun and stars; and the number 16. He is also associated with fire energy and may present in this manner to you. The stones that are believed to be connected to him are phantom quartz, rutilated quartz as well as any red or orange stone. He can also be associated with the stones, tiger's eye or tiger's iron.

He is a passionate angel and encourages us to be passionate about our healing work. If you are ready for your energy work to be ramped up, call in Archangel Nathaniel. If you are seeing a lot of red around you already, then it just might be him letting you know that you are prepared enough!

Chapter Eleven

Summary

Whew! I don't know about you, but I'm excited! Learning to talk to your angels just may be the single most important thing that you have ever done!

As you begin to receive your messages, you will notice that much of this divine communication concerns making changes that are in your best interest. As you make these changes, you will notice how good you feel and your overall mood will improve. Your life will feel more rewarding and your heart will be filled with love.

As you progress on your spiritual journey, other changes will naturally occur. Your sense of wonderment will increase and you will gravitate outdoors more. The grass will appear greener and the sky will seem bluer. You will find yourself listening to the quaint conversations of birds and the gentle rustling of the wind in the trees. You will see an enormous amount of beauty in everything around you. Worries will disappear and be replaced by an amazing sense of peace. You will be calm even in the face of adversity. Your happiness and positivity will radiate from your very being and influence everyone around you!

As I am finishing up this last page, I must say that I am hearing a familiar sound from the heavens. I recognize this amazing music as the joyous celebration of my angels after my healing. The difference here is that this celebration is not just for my completion of this book. *It is for you.* Your effort to connect with them is creating an enormous amount of energy and excitement that I can hear and actually feel within my physical body. To each of you, I will close with a message from the angels:

> *Listen carefully, my dear;*
> *For we are not that hard to hear.*
>
> *In the silence or in a song;*
> *We shall never lead you wrong.*
>
> *We will guide you every day with love;*
> *From all around and up above!*
>
> *Blessings!*
> *Cathy Catching*

Printed in the United States
By Bookmasters